The Contradiction of Christianity

DAVID E. JENKINS

The Contradiction of Christianity

SCM PRESS LTD

*Unless otherwise stated, biblical
quotations are from the Revised Version
of the Bible*

334 00246 X

First published 1976 by
SCM Press Ltd
26–30 Tottenham Road, London N1 4BZ
Second impression 1985

Printed in Great Britain by
Richard Clay (The Chaucer Press) Ltd
Bungay, Suffolk

Contents

Preface

This book arises out of the Edward Cadbury Lectures which I was invited to give at Birmingham University in 1974 and is published as the expanded version of these lectures. I am immensely grateful for the invitation given me, for the provocation to thinking and writing thus provided for me and for the warmth of the hospitality I received while giving the lectures. The book as a whole stands, therefore, as my response to the invitation and honour which the University of Birmingham offered to me.

In developing the theme and exposition of my lectures as well as adding some new material, I have made use of material I first worked out when I paid a visit to Melbourne in 1972 to give the Moorhouse Lectures after an invitation received through the Archbishop of Melbourne. I then gave six lectures under the general title of 'The Trinity – possibilities of God and Man'. The individual lectures were entitled:

I The Trinity: A vision of the divine reality and the human possibility

II History and experience: (*a*) The epistemological basis

III History and experience: (*b*) Trinity and personality

IV The kingdom of God and the body of Christ: (*a*) doctrine and social ethics

V The kingdom of God and the body of Christ: (*b*) community and individual

VI Prayer, poetry and practice

Moorhouse Lecture I, together with lectures IV and V, thus provided a first working through of some of the themes which I have further developed in these Cadbury lectures and material from them appears here and there throughout. When I came to develop the lectures into the book which now follows, I further found that Moorhouse lectures II and III filled out particularly glaring gaps in my exposition. The substance of Moorhouse lecture II therefore provided the main core for chapter 6 of this book, while Moorhouse lecture III appears largely in chapter 10. Hence I may perhaps be allowed to offer this book also as acknowledging my debt to those who invited me to Australia and as carrying forward the theological enterprise on which they helped me to embark.

D.E.J.

William Temple Foundation
Manchester
October 1975

Introduction

When you get from this introduction to the beginning of the book you will find that it starts with the word 'I'. My defence for this is twofold. First, the autobiographical element in doing theology seems inevitable. (On this, see further ch. 6 and especially pp. 80 ff.) Secondly, the book is about whether I am trapped in being me, whether every tribal 'we' is trapped in being an exclusive 'us' and whether there is any realistic hope of a way of being human which fulfils us all. So as well as being inevitable, it may turn out not to be too disastrously egotistical to start from autobiography.

This book, therefore, is some account of a continuing pilgrimage to find out what is offered in being human and what is involved in doing theology. In going on from attempting to do theology from Oxford University as a base to attempting to do theology from the base of the World Council of Churches in Geneva, the experience which has been most apparent to me has been the discovery of the extreme parochiality of 'myself' and of 'my theology'. On reflection, of course, this is what might be expected, but the obvious lies very well hidden until it is forced upon our attention. This discovery of the obvious having been made, however, it then became essential to pursue the question of the possible relations of this parochiality to any potential universality. This pursuit became all the more necessary as the increasing awareness of parochiality went along with an increasing perception of some humanly sinister features of it. What if my visions and hopes of being human and my visions and hopes from being a Christian were, in fact, totally contradicted? Hence the explorations which are described in what follows arise out of my pursuance of the tasks given to me as 'Director of Humanum Studies (Co-ordinator of Studies on Man)' at the World Council of Churches from July 1969 onwards. What these tasks were is sufficiently indicated for the purposes of this book in chapter 1.[1]

[1] For a fuller account see the report, *The Humanum Studies 1969–75*, ed. D. E. Jenkins, World Council of Churches, Geneva, 1975.

Given the variety of the new concepts encountered, new questions raised and new experiences undergone it becomes necessary to clear one's mind as to the situation in which one actually stands and as to the possibilities revealed in this situation. In one way this is a preliminary to getting on with the theological task and a preparation for developing one's human commitment. In another way, however, it is actually doing this task and developing this commitment. Presumably advancing in a pilgrimage is always both going on with it and preparing for the next stage of it.

I am most conscious of this ambiguity about doing a task and preparing for it in relation to my discussions about Marxism. For reasons given as the account develops, I have found it necessary to give a great deal of attention to Marxist analysis and Marxist intuitions. None the less I feel that what appears is mainly a clearing of the mind about Marxism and the advancing of some tentative theological reflections in response to Marxism. It is not yet a dialogue with Marxism. That requires situational involvement with human commitments being tested out and sought. In this connection, therefore, the work is simply preparatory.

In another connection, however, I hope that the work may represent some actual advance, however slight. In a postscript to my Bampton Lectures I wrote:

> The investigations of these lectures need to be followed up in relation to the social side of the life of men, and the things concerning Jesus need to be carefully scrutinized in relation to all those ways in which human togetherness is threatened, fails or never begins to be developed. We shall not be able to make satisfactory and effective sense of the cosmic significance of Jesus unless we develop and redevelop practical implications of the social significance of Jesus. The Kingdom of God stands for the fulfilment of the personal purposes of the universe in a perfected and perfecting society. I do not myself see effective sense being made of the theological and anthropological realities of the things concerning Jesus without commitment to the social and political dimensions of men's living.[2]

What follows reflects some wrestling with what is involved in 'commitment to the social and political dimension of men's living'.

The result seems to me to be rather like a series of more or less tentative sketches on a number of interlocking and interdependent subjects. The reason for attempting all of them together is the way in which they illuminate one another and depend on one another. The

[2] D. E. Jenkins, *The Glory of Man* (Bampton Lectures for 1966), SCM Press and Scribner 1967, p. 116.

tentativeness arises from the author's awareness of his partiality and of his limited perspective. Any boldness there is in some of the outlines arises, not from the confidence of the perceiver, but from confidence in the powers and the possibilities of what is perceived. If only one could sketch better, and respond more adequately to the demands and offers outlined!

I

Transcendence in the midst and the tribalism of Christian traditions and Christian theologies

I write as a Christian about the contradiction of Christianity. I do this with bewilderment and distress which often comes near to despair yet mingled with excitement and hope. For in this contradiction I find sources for renewed faith in God through Jesus and deeper hopes of being human through God and one another. The reader must judge for him- or herself into which category the argument which follows is to be placed. Perhaps it is that type of theological rationalization which attempts to twist necessity into the Procrustean mould of an obstinate faith which will not recognize its refutation. Or it could contain glimpses of an authentic theology which validly sees God in our conflicts and possibilities of growth in our failures. For myself, I do not suppose that I have clearly seen, accurately described or adequately responded to that about which I am attempting to write. But I am convinced that behind, in and through the flickers of light, the shadows of doubt and the distortions of man's inhumanity to man which provide the material for my reflections, it is possible to get to grips with and be gripped by the realities of God and the world. We are not dealing with the mere fantasies, exhilarations and fears of our own imaginations. We are offered, I believe, a gospel which not only overcomes gloom but also promises glory. But this offer is to be found not where we are confident and at ease but where we are contradicted and at a loss.

It is here, in the midst of what we actually feel, suffer, do and fail to do, that we can discover the possibilities of God which are, at the same time, the possibilities of being human. It was this sense of the discovery or rediscovery of God in the very midst of contradiction and confusion that led me to entitle the lectures which formed the original substance of this book 'Transcendence in the Midst' with the sub-title 'Concerning the Future of Man and the Freedom of God'. After I had completed the lectures I came to the conclusion that a more accurate indication of the particular perspective and motif of my enquiry was to be found in the idea of the contradiction of Christianity. The way to the understanding of God's transcendent presence in our midst and the way to the insights about the future promised to us human beings by God's freedom in and for history lies through the increasing awareness of the contradiction of Christianity. I must proceed therefore by indicating the interconnection of these themes and by trying to point to both the general drift and the general context of my argument.

For the context we may consider firstly the following quotation from Reinhold Niebuhr's *Moral Man and Immoral Society* which was published first in 1932, but is surely as relevant as ever to our present predicament:

> The insights of the Christian religion have become the almost exclusive possession of the more comfortable and privileged classes. These have sentimentalised them to such a degree, that the disinherited, who ought to avail themselves of their resources, have become so conscious of the moral confusions which are associated with them, that the insights are not immediately available for the social struggle in the Western World. If they are not made available, Western civilisation, whether it drifts toward catastrophe or gradually brings its economic life under social control, will suffer from cruelties and be harassed by animosities which destroy the beauty of human life. Even if justice should be achieved by social conflicts which lack the spiritual elements of non-violence, something will be lacking in the character of the society so constructed. There are both spiritual and brutal elements in human life. The perennial tragedy of human history is that those who cultivate the spiritual elements usually do so by divorcing themselves from or misunderstanding the problems of collective man, where the brutal elements are most obvious. These problems therefore remain unsolved, and force clashes with force, with nothing to mitigate the brutalities or eliminate the futilities of the social struggle.[1]

Another and more specific way into an understanding of the contradiction of Christianity is well illustrated by some words of Dr Buthelezi, the distinguished Black Lutheran theologian from South Africa, as reported in an article in *The Guardian* of 24 December 1973:

> God will ask: 'Black man, where were you when the white man abandoned my gospel and went to destruction?' When the black man answers, 'I was only a Kaffir – who could I dare preach to, my baas?',

[1] *Moral Man and Immoral Society*, reissued Scribner 1960, SCM Press 1963, p. 255.

God will say: 'Was Christ's resurrection not sufficient to liberate you, black man, from that kind of spiritual and psychological death? Go to eternal condemnation, black man, for you did not muster courage enough to save your white brother!' Ours is a Christianity in caricature. It seems that the white man, as the main architect of the South African way of life, has done his best to destroy the heart of the faith he brought with him.

This is the situation I wish to face – the context I want to take seriously – the cruel caricatures of Christianity which we have produced, which have forced others into caricatures of their own, and which call the whole of Christianity into question. I see what I am attempting as an exercise in 'White Theology', indeed in white bourgeois English theology. I wish to follow up a suggestion of Manalo Radel, a Philippine theologian, when he writes: 'The question is not: "How can we adapt theology to our needs?" Rather, how can our needs create a theology which is our own?'[2] It is well known that some of those Christians who have become aware of the full force of white racism upon themselves, the contexts of their lives and the pressures of their immediate past have felt the urgent need consciously to develop *Black* Theology. Other Christians in other parts of the world are seeing that as their cultures emerge from the domination of the West so their reflections on, and understandings of, the Christian faith require also to emerge from Western patterns into something more authentically their own. The struggle for this authentic 'theology which is our own' is a risky and ambiguous one. As the quotation from Radel suggests, it is perfectly possible to 'adapt theology to our needs' and so dissolve any transcendent or potentially universal reference into the temporary particularities of the current way of seeing the problems of the moment. But it is also possible, and it is certainly necessary, to struggle for a theology, that is to say an understanding of God and man through Jesus Christ, which emerges in the midst of a serious attempt to respond to the needs and hopes of being human as they are experienced in any particular cultural or national area. It will be necessary, at other points in the argument of this book, to return to the problems and possibilities of developing a theology which is both 'our own' and also responsible and responsive to revelation and to universal potentiality, if there be such. Meanwhile, however, I simply wish to make this point that I am aware that I am attempting to work out some theological discoveries prompted by a very particular situation and set of pressures. In this I am consciously

[2] 'The Theologian at Work, Philippines 1970–80s. A Suggestion', *Philippine Studies* 3, 1971.

attempting to respond like other groups of Christians elsewhere. My particular intention is to investigate whether we, as white English or British Christians, can receive an awareness of our limitations and distortions which liberates our Christianity rather than distorts, condemns and contradicts its universal significance.

In the face of caricatures and contradiction we have to ask whether there is a gospel extending to all men – an offer of wholeness and fulfilment which is truly total. But we have to ask this with a full awareness of the limitations of us who ask. Hence we have to theologize for ourselves in mutual awareness of the views of others and with mutual accountability between Christians of different circumstances and perspectives. This challenge is the concern of the whole book but the immediate point is the situational challenge to *my* Christianity. That is to say the way I am contradicted as a Christian by certain aspects of my being white and by certain features of the Church of England of which I am a member.

But I do not experience my position as a defensive one. This of course can be established in exposition and practice only and through the judgment of others. However, I see and feel the situation as follows. 'My Christianity' is challenged to its very roots and existence by the Third World and the poor and marginals in our own societies. As I shall argue, especially in chapters 3 and 4, this challenge is given great point and effect with the help of insights derived from Marx. But that to which 'my Christianity' points and of which it gives me glimpses challenges absolutely everything – with what, at the moment, I shall refer to simply as 'an exceeding weight of glory'. (This will be especially the concern of the last part of the book.)

Thus, as far as I can understand myself, my basic wish and will is *not* to defend 'my Christianity' but to find presently appropriate ways of following Jesus, of receiving the truth as it is in Christ Jesus and of being found in him which, in my understanding, is to be led into God and into all things. Thus the context of the book – and so, necessarily, much of the content – is this challenge to the understanding and the existence of Christian faith which is presented by the increasing awareness that the church of the gospel does not practise the gospel. Rather it shares in the practices of exploitation, dominance and indifference which are common in those societies where the church has largely lived and preached. These sentiments are commonplace to some, while to others they may seem simply the ill-considered echoing of the rhetoric of 'the left'. We should not however take for granted either the self-evident truth or the obvious exaggeration and falsity of this challenge.

At the moment I am simply indicating what I propose to investigate and hope to establish.

Our starting question then is 'In what situation do we theologize – and how are we to theologize about it?' For me the most important contextual feature of our situation is this direct and total challenge to our Christianity, to which I am briefly pointing in a preliminary way. But the *content* which I am concerned to theologize about is neither fundamentally nor finally this challenge. It is rather a content concerned with the future of man and a reflection about what it means to be human. The basic question remains not 'Can Christianity be saved?' but 'What human salvation and fulfilment is there in Jesus Christ?' Or, rather, the *basic* question, as I hope to show, is something like 'Is there any hope of anything that could be realistically called human salvation and fulfilment?' My position is that Jesus Christ remains of central significance both to the possibility of answering that question positively and to the content which such an answer can have. But it is difficult to do justice to the paradoxical reality of the situation which I am attempting to describe.

The contradiction of Christianity is real. The phrase is not a manner of speaking. Our behaviour as Christians and the performance of the institutions of Christianity have been such as to deprive us of the right to be Christians or to expect credibility for what Christianity stands for. Further this is not a mere matter of definition (for example, some version of the argument that 'real' Christianity is the following of Jesus Christ and most 'Christians' do not 'really' follow him). Real Christianity is quite clearly what Christians actually do and are together with the institutions which they in fact have. (In history no other realities exist.) If these historical existences, events and institutions are of such a quality that they contradict the claims, hopes and visions which are stated to be both the basis for and the aims of Christian believing, then Christianity is, in fact, contradicted. And this I both believe and feel to be the case. But I also feel and believe that there is a vital sense in which God, in and through Jesus, speaks and is active precisely through and in this contradiction. To understand, glimpse or hope this is not to transcend the contradiction, and the historical facts which constitute the contradiction in some neat, satisfying and soothing synthesis. We have no syntheses and things do not fit. The Transcendence is in *the midst*. In the midst, that is to say, of real contradictions and completely disturbing misfits and distortions which threaten our faith and life with actual nonsense and undermine our hopes and visions with incipient and often vivid despair.

Perhaps, therefore, I should not have written in the opening sentences of this book about 'the argument' of it. For I do not believe that my theme nor the discoveries which permit it lend themselves to exposition in an extended and coherent argument like a treatise. There are, of course, many arguments at many points. But the overall effect I am aiming at is rather the description of a discovery which promises much more to be discovered. And this discovery does not build up out of a series of contradictions overcome, paradoxes resolved and problems neatly settled. It is, rather, an experienced way of receiving comprehension, direction and hope in the midst of the contradictions, paradoxes and problems. For a Christian, to face the contradiction of Christianity is not to indulge in shadow-boxing about a nicely posed verbal problem. It is to live with the possibility that he is living with, from and by a lie.

It may not be possible to maintain in discursive writing the tension between contradiction and creativity, between distortion of reality and revelation of reality, which seems to be inherent in actual living, searching and believing. It is certainly possible to experience great clarity and excitement of vision while at the same time being acutely aware that the vision is threatened and the clarity is denied. But I at any rate cannot write in such a multi-dimensional way. Hence it is possible to proceed only by a series of descriptions and arguments which must gain their fuller meaning, if any, from their interrelationships and from the contexts which they provide for one another. We live in the midst of all this and much more. The realities and possibilities of our lives are not to be reduced to the one line or perspective or dimension of any one argument or description. But the arguments or descriptions have to be taken one at a time in the hope that a cumulative effect may develop. I continue therefore with my description of what has led me to see Christianity, or at least my Christianity, as contradicted.

The main source for the materials and experiences on which I am now drawing lies in the work I have been doing with the World Council of Churches as their so-called Director of Humanum Studies or Coordinator of Studies on Man. This is a post invented at the Uppsala Assembly 1968 and intended to work towards the Nairobi Assembly 1975. A freelance theologian without departmental responsibilities was appointed to hold a watching brief, and perhaps to act as 'agent provocateur', on the wide range of issues arising in the area of what is happening to man, of how this affects Christian faith and of how the Christian faith should respond.

The effect of working in such a post full-time for four years and then part-time after that is exposure to an unusual multiplicity of issues, perspectives and traditions. This, of course, does not make me 'an authority'. It does, however, pose many questions about the perspectives within which and the bases upon which we customarily think and act. For there is the opportunity and necessity of working with people of widely different perspectives and assumptions. Thus one is given an acute experience of the plurality of views, understandings and approaches which men and women exercise or assume in their approach to living and believing. Together with this one becomes equally acutely aware of how conditioned our understanding and judging is. Our differing perspectives and situations are themselves both conditioned and conditioning factors and influences on us. Hence, any such attempt as the Humanum Studies of the WCC has not only to face up to the question 'What is man?' or perhaps better the question 'Who are we and what hope do we have of becoming what?' There is also the question – What is the relation of the 'we' who are asking the question to the 'we' of the human race? Indeed, is there any hope or prospect of a common 'we' developing at all or being experienced at all? On every important human issue one is faced with evidence of fragmentation and of conflict which seems to point in the direction of human meaningless-ness. All of which from a Christian point of view provides another sharp challenge to the claim and the hope about a universal gospel.

Therefore there is a challenge to Christian faith from plurality and diversity which reinforces the challenge from identification with in-justice and oppression. On the other hand, the question of what it is or might be to be or to become human and the question of whether there is a universal gospel remains closely interwoven. We remain, therefore, with the question about the salvation and fulfilment which is offered to human beings 'in Jesus Christ' in the midst of contexts and situations which challenge Christianity to its very roots. At least, this is where *I* remain and remain hopefully. For I cannot separate the challenges which appear to deny my Christian faith from the very meaning and hope which that faith seems to be offering me and to all men. The studies and experiments which have heightened my awareness of how 'my Christianity' is compromised, contradicted, limited, partial, and therefore on so many grounds apparently and plausibly false, have, at the same time, directed and re-directed to truth, gospel and hope in and in connection with Jesus and with his God and Father and with his Holy Spirit. The source of Christian faith can be discovered to be affirming himself in the very challenges, contradictions and conflicts which are undermining Christianity or, at any rate, the Christianity to which I belong.

For us white bourgeois Christians this situation can be quite fairly described as a judgment of death which, as always in the will and love of God, is an offer to receive repentance and resurrection. It is for this reason, the reason that nothing less than death and resurrection is involved, that one of the following chapters is entitled 'Radical spirituality and radical politics'. The radical judgment and radical renewal that are offered to us are also possibilities which are offered to and needed by all men, in the forms which are appropriate to their differing conditions and circumstances. Hence in facing up to the challenges to our Christianity in all its particularities, failures and limitations we can discover and rediscover something of the potential universality of the offer of God in Jesus. There is the opportunity to discover in new and deepened ways that human possibilities and fulfilment lie in the freedom of God, that is to say in the infinite freedom which God is and in the inexhaustible freedom which God offers.

This freedom, this being, this activity of God is a mystery which goes well beyond description. Truth here is not something which we can grasp but rather that of which we may know ourselves to be a part. Hence it is as inappropriate, even blasphemous, to offer a definition of what it means to be human as it is to set out a description of God. However, if the Mystery is indeed related to the meaning and fulfilment of what it is to be human, then it must be possible to speak of visions, experiences and hopes which point to it or to the effects and possibilities of it. Similarly, the truth which is to be lived in rather than taken hold of must have indications arising from it which point to forms and ways of living out of and into this truth. It is pursuit of these indications through perceptions of contradiction which form the substance of this book.

In this pursuit, as has already been hinted, the phrase 'transcendence in the midst' seems most useful as a focus for the indications and pointers being gathered about this Mystery of the freedom of God and these possibilities of being human. In particular, it stresses that it is *in the midst* of challenges, conflicts and betrayals that God is to be known. It is to be hoped, perhaps against hope, that the phrase will not become a tired slogan or a label for that which, because it has been explained, has been explained away. Both the 'Transcendence' and the 'in the midst' should retain their full value, whatever that may be. That is to say at least that 'Transcendence' must refer to that which can be fully contained under no circumstances and in no run, however long, while 'in the midst' must always refer to a human 'here and now' or a collection of them. We have to investigate and reflect on this quality and power of going beyond every present possibility and every present obstacle which is present in, available to, and yet not contained by, all human beings, their situations and their affairs.

Thus the theme of Transcendence in the midst is the linking theme between the facing of the contradiction of Christianity and the glimpsing of the possibilities for the future of man to be expected from the reality of the freedom of God. This is the preliminary interweaving of the three themes from which I started. The possibility of Transcendence in the midst of the contradiction of Christianity is also the possibility that there is saving and fulfilling power present in all human situations and for all human beings. The way in to this central discovery, which is the theme to be explored throughout the book, lies through a subsidiary reflection about the form which our contradiction of Christianity has assumed. This form is characterized by the phrase which I have used as the second half of the title of this chapter, namely, 'The Tribalism of Christian Traditions and Christian Theologies.'

This notion of 'tribalism' is important because it provides a way of handling both the difficulty which is my starting-point and the difficulty of my starting-point. The difficulty which is my starting-point is the contradiction of Christianity. (Truly a difficulty for a Christian!) But the difficulty of my starting-point is that I face this contradiction of Christianity as a Christian. This is to say that the basis on which I both perceive this contradiction and start to attempt to respond to it is in fact Christian believing and Christian community now, in all the particularity of their various contradictory and contradicted manifestations.

Thus I do not get my other two themes of 'Transcendence in the midst' and 'The freedom of God and the future of man' from nowhere in particular or from somewhere in general. The uses of such phrases together with the experiences of the world and of human living, and the interpretation offered for the world and for human living which these phrases indicate, are not uses, experiences and interpretations which arise randomly or without their specific context and presuppositions. The whole approach derives from the context of the Christian church and the presuppositions of the Christian faith. It is this Christian church and this Christian faith, particularly in the forms which I inherit and in which I participate, that are now seen to be in a context of conflict, contradiction, limitedness and plurality. Nevertheless, the basis in history and in human experiencing for that knowledge of God as both the present help and the future fulfilment of man which is offered in Jesus Christ is that community, or rather those communities, who have declared and handed on their belief in the God and Father of Jesus

Christ through the Spirit. They form the only starting-point for discovering this gospel, if gospel it is. But this starting-point is challenged to the point of destruction, certainly to the point of implausibility and incredibility. The starting-point of my explanation and exposition thus becomes these very challenges and what they show, both about the failures and futilities of the church and about the resources and possibilities of the gospel which created the church and about the God who is the only source and end of that gospel. It is these challenges and the creative aspect of them that can be helpfully illuminated by considering how they throw into relief the 'tribalism' of our Christian traditions and practices.

Thus I see the line of my discovery developing as follows. The starting-point of the vision of the possibilities of being human lies within the Christian faith and church and, as I have already indicated and shall try to show further in the course of my argument, this starting-point remains indispensable. But, this starting-point, the starting-point of a Christian within the Christian faith and church, clearly contradicts itself and falsifies its gospel by the very forms and processes of existence which Christian faith, Christian life and Christian church have taken on and which they continue to display. However it is possible to see that this conflict and contradiction between the possibilities and promises of a given identity with its forms of existence and the pathologies which develop as these are lived out constitute the crucial problem of human existence and the definitive threat to our human future. In other words, the limiting and distorting tribalism by which Christians preserve and attempt to pass on their understandings of what it is to be Christian reflect and can throw light on the limiting and distorting expressions of human identity which produce man's inhumanity to man and threaten to reduce human living to self-destruction. In fact, tribalism is a fundamental human problem – nowhere more manifest than in the behaviour and institutions of white bourgeois English Christians. But it is by no means confined to such tribes and groups. It is a critical area in both the health and the pathology of human identity. Throughout our discussions we shall find it necessary to reflect on what sort of 'belonging' is open to human beings and as to how far the developing of identity depends on conflict or on collaboration. Meanwhile, by expanding and clarifying the use of the term 'tribalism' we can complete this stage of our investigation, with reference to Christian traditions and theologies.

First, the term 'tribalism' is chosen precisely because this is an exercise in white bourgeois theology. 'Tribalism' has been something generally decried by persons of Western culture and held to be a limiting feature of 'primitive' societies. Black men for example are 'tribal'. Civilized modern men are not. This tendency in usage is itself a strong indication of the negative side of various forms of white tribalism. People outside our tribes are neither so civilized nor so human as we are but subject to 'tribal' limitations. I choose the term 'tribalism', therefore, to provoke and evoke a sharp reassessment of our self-understanding vis-à-vis those who are very different from us.

Secondly, I choose the term because the advantages and disadvantages of tribalism are being reassessed. This is being done both by so-called outsiders and observers of tribal living and, more importantly, by those who have been identified with a generally admitted way of tribal living, such as Africans, American Indians and Australian Aborigines. There is a reaffirmation and rediscovery of the human value of a clearly defined idiosyncratic culture, of the mutual support and responsibility of a tribal structure, and of corporateness as a starting-point which is preferable to that of a fragmented individuality. Thus 'tribalism' is a term which can usefully be employed to draw attention to the part played by 'belonging' in having an identity and in being human. Since human beings are particular and limited it may well be that the particularity and limitations of being tribal, or something like them, are necessary for the process of becoming human to begin.

In any case, 'tribalism' is a term which is chosen because it raises necessary questions about human identity, belonging and becoming. It thus has very positive aspects and leaves the way open for a reassessment of the possible proper values of the tribalism of Christian theologies and traditions, once they are recognized, assessed for what they are and subjected to judgment, repentance and renewal. It may be that tribal theologies are not necessarily destructive of being Christian and that tribal ways of living are not necessarily destructive of being human and of the human future.

On the other hand the tenor of what has been written so far has, I hope, indicated that the term 'tribalism' is used with at least a negative resonance. This brings me to my third reason for choosing the term. 'Tribalism' refers to a strictly limited awareness of identity which can easily have destructive effects. In his small book *Man's Nature and his Communities* Niebuhr remarks: 'The chief source of man's inhumanity to man seems to be the tribal limits of his sense of obligation to other men.'[3] This draws attention to a central critical issue about being and

[3] *Man's Nature and his Communities*, Scribner 1965, Geoffrey Bles 1966, p. 63.

becoming human and about the prospects for the future of men. We may ask 'When is a man not a man ?' or better, for this is too masculine a formulation – 'When is a human being not a human being ?' The answer deduced from much human behaviour is 'When he or she is not one of us'. The tribal 'we-group' which regards 'us' as the norm for human behaviour, judgment and action is at the centre of the problem of the pathology of human identity with which we must be much concerned if we are investigating the meaning of being human and the future of man.

Of course 'tribalism' is being used in an extended sense in the discussion. As Niebuhr puts it in the discussion already referred to, 'The distinguishing marks of tribalism may consist of common racial origins, or language, or religion and culture or class.' Thus the term is being extended from a technical anthropological term referring to a certain defined type of human social organization. I think, however, that this is quite legitimate, and indeed justified by the actual ambiguities of the phenomenon itself. In particular it is useful to draw attention to the fact that *that by which we identify ourselves and have our sense of identity, significance and belonging is also that by which we dehumanize others.* This is a diagnosis which is central to the way of seeing things which this book is concerned to reflect.

Christian tribalism partakes of all the three features referred to. It demonstrates condescension, arrogance and indifference to 'lesser breeds without the law', it is necessarily related to identity, and it is exercised in dehumanizing ways. The localization and participation of a vision, experience and understanding of the Christian faith is erected into a universal way of seeing the world and men and then used to justify, permit or ignore attacks on others, indifference to them and domination over them. 'Me and my group' in our self-understanding are held to be the universal norm of both humanity and salvation. The attitudes and behaviour which follow from this are both dehumanizing and destructive of the very message of salvation from which the original identity was drawn.

For evidence supporting this understanding of Christian tribalism we may return to the quotation already given (p. 7) from Dr Buthelezi: 'Ours is a Christianity of caricature. It seems that the white man, as the main architect of the South African way of life, has done his best to destroy the heart of the faith he brought with him.' We may also consider Marx's criticism of the Christian religion as simply an ideology emanating from specific social and historical structures. (For a discussion of Marx's criticism of Christianity see pp. 106 ff.). There is also a growing mass of evidence to be derived from much Christian writing drawing attention to the destructive and oppressive effects of the tribal limitations and assumptions in Western theological traditions and the practices of Western church structures, writing especially, although not exclusively, to be found in the non-Western world. These writings include much discussion among Latin American writers and theologians, often greatly influenced by Marxism, and the writings of Black theologians in the USA. More and more writing is also emerging from Africa, with a 'Black theology' that is not that of the USA. In the Philippines and other parts of South-East Asia Christian writers and thinkers wrestle with the problems of 'a theology which is our own'. In India there is a wide range of theological reflection, written both in English and in the vernacular languages, against the background of deep attempts to respond to the authenticity of long-established cultures and philosophies. A further major challenge to all Western tribalisms comes from China and from the reflections which the thought and experiences of Communist China are provoking among those who live directly within her immediate spheres of influence. A rather different but equally significant exposure of the limitations of Christian thinking and understanding hitherto comes from the writings concerning Women's Liberation. From all these areas the highly limited and conditioned nature of what has hitherto been taken as normative Christian thinking and acting is thrown into relief.

Thus the critical question becomes whether Marx is altogether right – that Christianity is nothing but an ideology emanating from specific social and historical structures, or whether, as many Third World Christians believe and argue, Marx serves to draw our attention to the ideological, cultural and, as I would say, tribal conditioning of expressions of Christianity. But if these conditionings are recognized for what they are, then liberation can be received so that the message of the gift of God and of the infinite possibilities of man once more emerges to be a human gospel indeed.

It is my understanding that this latter possibility exists because of the reality of Transcendence in the midst, of the presence and action of the God who again and again overthrows the limitations of both individual and social human pathology and who is, mercifully, too much for both the tribalisms of Christianity and the determinisms of Marxism.

2

Human identity and Christian identity

It turns out, then, that I am trying to look at the human dilemma from the point of view of the Christian dilemma. This inevitably involves me in looking at the dilemma of my sort of human beings within the whole human situation from the point of view of my sort of Christians. Hence, this is an exercise in white bourgeois English theology. My problem is 'How do we respond to the inevitable relativizing of our perspectives?' This problem is acute for me as a Christian because Christianity proclaims a universal gospel and is compounded for me as a white bourgeois Christian because of the identification of my church with structures and institutions of particular oppression. I claim to believe in a universal gospel on the basis of a community manifesting narrow and often dehumanizing tribalism.

Why, then, do I not get rid of at least one layer or level of my dilemma by divesting myself of my Christian faith and my Christian community?

Because to do so would be a final act of despair about the possibilities of human being and human identity. It would also be a betrayal of a vision of human being and becoming which is unsurpassable in both its completeness and its warmth. Finally, it would be a repudiation of a Giver, a Giving and a Gift known and to some extent shared in. I may, perhaps, explain what I mean by these last remarks if I go on as follows.

The dilemma which is in one way troubling me and in another way exciting me is a peculiarly Christian one. It does not spring simply from the failure of Christianity, but also from the implications of the truth of the Christian gospel. (This, incidentally, is why, as I have already written, I do not regard this exercise as a defensive means of protecting the plausibility of Christianity, but as an explanatory means of extending our response to the living Truth from which the Christian gospel proceeds and to which it points.)

The Christian gospel proclaims that God is – that he is as he is in Jesus – and that therefore there is hope of, and hope in, being human. Or, as Fr Gustavo Gutierrez puts it, 'To announce the Gospel is to proclaim that the love of God is present in the historical becoming of mankind.'[1] Because of what the Christian knows 'through Jesus Christ' he or she also knows that it is both a proper question and an exciting question to ask about human identity, human being and human becoming. It is also a question to be asked both about all men and about each and every man, woman and child. For in this Christian understanding, vision, gospel, there is no contradiction between universality and particularity. My being human is to be fulfilled and find its meaning in the being human of all mankind.

This is so because to be human is the gift of God. This is what Jesus Christ enables us to believe and offers us the chance to practice – that being human has a source, a potentiality and a fulfilment which is given by God, offered by God and secured by God. Therefore being human is not solely at the mercy of time, circumstances and death. We can be saved and fulfilled.

The Bible in its main themes, and in the major stories and pictures which give shape to its message, not only supports but actually puts forward this understanding of the gift of God to men so that they might be all that they might be. The main traditional understandings developed in the Christian churches likewise in differing ways and despite the immense distortions in practice also reflect this. The conviction is that man depends upon God for being man and that therefore he can have the highest possible hopes of his humanity. This biblical and this traditional understanding has both its focus and its climax in Jesus who is believed to be the reality of God existing as the reality of that which is human.

This Christian knowledge that to be human is the gift of God is, in the Christian understanding, itself a gift. That men have this high calling and these divine potentialities is not a deduction but a revelation. That is to say that the Christian does not deduce the basic answer to the question 'What is man?' nor to the question 'What is salvation?' These answers are given to him. This giving, for its fulfilment, lies not only in the past but also in the present and in the future. The first and fundamental point lies, however, in the giving, discovered in history, renewed in history and to be fulfilled beyond history. This giving is believed to be God at work or, better still, in this giving God is known. We may even say that to know the giving is to know God.

I should like to reflect a little further on the language used here. I do not say: 'To know the *gift* is to know God.' I say: 'To know the giving

[1] *A Theology of Liberation*, Orbis Books, New York, 1973, SCM Press 1974, p. 268.

is to know God.' I do not want a pure object or thing-word which refers to the result of an activity or the detachable effect of an action. I require a word which expresses action itself, which conveys the notion of the presence of energy and which cannot be separated from whoever or whatever is acting, is energizing, is present. This choice of words is called for because God is not deduced from his gifts. He is known in his giving. This is of fundamental importance with regard to the Christian understanding of, and sharing in, the present struggles to be human, that is, to achieve freedom from oppression, from physical degradation and from being overwhelmed in an environment seemingly out of control. It is, in fact, about Transcendence in the midst.

In view of the need to face up to the limitations of our tribalisms it could be of great value to investigate how far and in what way the idea that I am expressing in the form 'God is known in his giving' could be expressed in, say, Malayalam or Chinese or in an African idiom, in French, German and Spanish or in Russian and Greek, and so on. But this is beyond my personal capacity so that I must confine myself to drawing attention to the need for a sensitivity to the partiality and limitations of language. We are discussing the meaning of salvation as Christians envisage it and thus the relation between human identity and Christian identity. But while the meanings are ours (we have to do the speaking, seek the understanding and take responsibility for proclamation and sharing) the salvation is of God. This is the basis behind all meanings which alone gives them power. Further, since salvation is indeed of God it is addressed to, and concerned with, all men, past, present and future and absolutely without exception. For God is the ultimate reality who embraces all reality absolutely without exception. Yet the universality of the salvation cannot be matched by a corresponding universality in the meanings apprehended, expressed or commended. For meanings have to be expressed in language which is of a particular time, place and culture and meanings have to be apprehended in the lives of men lived out in a particular time, place and culture. Thus here we come back to our dilemma about the belief in a universal gospel on the basis of a community sharing a narrow and often dehumanizing tribalism.

But this very problem and paradox of the meaning of salvation for Christians points also to the unique reality and power of salvation as Christians believe it to be offered. For Christians believe that salvation is, ultimately, the giving of God himself to men so that their humanity is infinitely filled and fulfilled. ('To be human is the gift of God.') But the uniquely Christian understanding of this giving of God is that provided by Jesus Christ, himself seen, received and understood against the stories of God's dealings with men reflected in the Old Testament scriptures. Thus there is no contradiction between the universality, infinitude and absoluteness of God and his giving himself in, through and to historical particularities. Jesus Christ is the decisive evidence offered to the faith of Christians and for the faith of Christians. He confirms to us that the activity of God himself ensures that particular moments, historical processes and embodied persons are the places where God is met, known, received and responded to. This activity of God is his universal and all-embracing work of bringing about salvation, that is, union with him and with all fulfilled things and persons in him.

For all human beings who must live here and now and in particular, the ultimate enjoyment of all this fullness of his salvation lies always in the future but it is likewise always in each human here and now that God's giving of himself is to be received and known. There is no other human place for receiving the gift of salvation than where we now are. How could there be? For we have nowhere else to be and to become human than where we now are, whether, for us, being human is a tragedy, a joy, a nonsense, a bore or a routine. Thus in the Christian understanding of salvation, whatever particular meanings are found or expressed, there is no necessary contradiction between the universality of salvation (the gift of God himself to enable man to be human) and the limitations of particular meanings and expressions about salvation. Rather there is, potentially, richness. For, first, this particularity is the way God gives himself to men, for it is in this particularity that men live and develop (or are distorted) as men. And, secondly, God's commitment to these particularities of history show that it is in and through history that he is building up the ultimate richness of what it is to be human. This is the biblical pattern of God's dealing with men in their history for a fulfilment which goes beyond history.

In this steady work of giving himself to men God has built up in history a people who have come to know him in this work and to know him as the one who does this work. The record of this building up of a people who receive the knowledge of God and develop this knowledge in a continued dealing with God is reflected in the writings of the Old Testament. Here a series of patterns and pictures and stories is offered to us. People discover who they are and how their history makes sense and how they are to make sense of their history (what they can be and what they must do) through encounters with him who offers identity, sense and purpose in the midst of events.

Abraham, Moses and the prophets discover themselves, their God and the role and possibilities of their people together in the demands and offers of events and circumstances. Similarly the people discover themselves, their God and their future together in circumstances such as those that lie behind the story of the Exodus. The continuing thread in history is the people, with their tradition and understandings building up out of their history. But the people themselves (or prophetic and gifted men working in and through the life of the people) discover that the continuing thread is a continuing and faithful reality and activity who is at work among them, through them and for them. They are in fact discovering and receiving their identity *in the midst* of their history.

But there can be no question of this creative and saving activity and reality being identified with them or confined to them. He is not at their disposal or under their control. Rather they depend for their identity and future on him. As their history develops so they learn that 'he' who is in the midst of them is also over against them in disturbance, overthrow and judgment in order to reshape them and renew them for their future and their fulfilment. Likewise they come to recognize 'him' as at work quite as much in the history from which they suffer (e.g., Cyrus is 'his anointed', Isa. 45.1) as in the history to which they contribute.

It is necessary to refer to this continuing and faithful reality and activity as 'he' and as 'God' in order to be able to speak at all. But it is also necessary to remember that who 'he' is and therefore what the word 'God' refers to is not something that we mean or intend but always something that he reveals. The Old Testament never offers a firm grasp on the identity of God (we do not know who he is in himself, we are not able to know his name) nor is there clear knowledge in advance of precisely what he will do (he is discovered in and by means of troubling and unexpected events in and after their happening). But what the Old Testament does bear witness to is a steadily built up assurance that he always will be, and that he will always act consistently with himself in his work of saving and fulfilling his people. There is, therefore, sustained faith in him and an established expectation of him.

Christians are constituted by the discovery that it is Jesus who embodies this faithful expectation, is the living embodiment in history of the kingdom of God. Therefore the Christian vision of salvation, of the full possibilities of Christian and human identity, has always been sought and seen in the light of the records of the discovery of the saving God reflected in the Old Testament; and in the light of the witness to the embodiment of this saving God in Jesus which is contained in the New Testament. There is no valid or powerful meaning which can be given to salvation which is independent of and out of touch with these records. Salvation depends upon God and we are dependent upon God for our saving knowledge of his saving work. It is to the discovery of this work which these records point. But what Christians can and do mean by salvation and human fulfilment is not *settled* by these records. The meaning of salvation cannot be finally settled until it is fully and finally enjoyed. That is to say until men are fulfilled in their being human through receiving the fullness of the life of God in unimpeded relations with him and with one another. Christian identity cannot be fully discovered or completed until human identity is fully enjoyed. It is the mistaken conversion of this open promise of identity into a narrowly defined and jealously guarded tribalism which has been and is the source of much of the contradiction of Christianity.

We do not know what this final coincidence of Christian identity and human identity will mean, i.e., what it will be like, what sort of experience it will be. Meanwhile, however, we are concerned with meanings and actions in our present particularities, struggles and hopes. Here we have the opportunity of receiving in our turn and for our times the discovery of who we are and how we are to be and become human. This involves discovering how our history makes sense and how we are to act to make sense of our history through encounters with him who offers identity, sense and purpose in the midst of events. We have our opportunities of learning and practising how being human is the gift of God.

I hope this immediately preceding discussion makes clear why I cannot give up the dilemma produced by the contradiction between the particular experiences of Christianity embodied in myself, my church and my Western tradition of Christianity and the vision and gospel of Jesus Christ. It may also offer some hints, to be developed in the further course of our exploration, as to why I see the challenge and disturbance of this dilemma as the very stimulus to the way forward. For this is a way forward into breaking out of a restricted and distorting Christian and human identity towards a broader and more open identity which is on its way towards the one new man in Jesus Christ which will be the fulfilment of all.

So to ignore this very disturbing dilemma or, under its apparent contradiction and threat, to abandon Christian church, faith and gospel would be to repudiate a Giver, Giving and Gift already at least partially known. Moreover, such an abandonment would suggest that one was arrogantly and ignorantly identifying God and his giving with what I and my fellows make of his gifts. It would thus be one more example of what might be called tribalistic idolatry which identifies what I and mine have made a norm or practised as normative with the definitive symbols of ultimate reality and worth. It would also be to betray a vision of human being and becoming which is unsurpassable both in its completeness and in its warmth. For the vision takes its shape from the basic assurance of a loving relationship with the God who is love and who expresses this in and as the outgoing identification and committed suffering of Jesus. The vision therefore speaks of an energy oriented towards man, an energy who has the resources to enable all to love all at the cost and with the glory that this entails.

The meaning and the fulfilment which is promised is not therefore intellectual, political, historical or metaphysical – a fitting into a scheme and an activity which somehow justifies and occupies but does not satisfy. Rather the fulfilment is human, face to face and of mutual enjoyment – a community of communion which is glimpsed by lovers, poets and all men and women who know, however briefly, that to give all is to be all and receive all. This is the community which both is and requires eternity because of the inexhaustible possibilities which all can give to each and each can draw from all. It will be where what love has glimpsed is fulfilled by love.

But such a vision, a promise and an aim forces one very close to, if not into the heart of, despair. This is why to turn aside from the Christian dilemma either by ignoring its full force or by rejecting Christian faith and church would be a final act of despair about the possibilities of human being and human identity. For once one has seen that if love is love then nobody can be fully human unless and until everyone is fully human, what then ? Love says that every human being is absolutely valuable and the potential whole is totally valuable. And we, at least we who are Christians, cannot turn away from this, for this is the gospel of Immanuel, of God with us. And in this the gospel surely confirms and echoes, as well as creates, widespread intuitions and hopes of human solidarity. But that this seemingly makes love unbearable is made clear enough by the necessarily dulling effect of the Oxfam poster, for instance, or the TV 'war on famine' programme. It is not possible to be fully open to the human potentiality and actuality, together with the futility and suffering, which is there portrayed. Yet to reflect on even one example of such things is to reinforce our awareness of being faced with that which is unbearable. A picture which caught my eye and, for a moment, focused my attention was one put out at the time of a famine in Bengal. A father was carrying the body of his daughter into the river where it was to be abandoned to the waters. Her hair was hanging down over his arm in a pattern which reminded me of the way

I have often seen my daughter's hair. My daughter was warm, well-fed and alive. His daughter was cold, starved and dead. And this is unbearable. This is human misery which is not to be denied. The anguish and the outrage of this seems to be a fundamental and an intolerable intuition which cannot be turned aside or assuaged either by rage about the iniquities of a capitalist distribution system or by intensive activity on behalf of a voluntary committee for overseas aid and development. Both these may be necessary but nothing will cancel out the outrage.

Moreover one knows even more intimately that love is unbearable. It does not take very much sensitivity or perceptivity to be aware, at least from time to time, that my own practice does not measure up to the love I have for those closest to me, let alone to the love they show for me. In a paradoxical way love creates demands because it reveals possibilities and this combination of demand and possibility tends to situations, the full implications of which are unbearable, precisely because one is not confronted with an imposition or a duty which can be rejected or denied. To miss or distort such an opportunity is to distort everything, including oneself. But it is often done.

But perhaps we are spared the unbearable nature of love because it is so clearly impossible, in the total and all-inclusive sense pointed to by the vision and the gospel. In practice all our loving, caring, and indignation against obstacles to and contradictions of loving and caring, are so clearly selective; selected moreover by our conditioning and circumstances and selected because they are appropriate to our needs. We have neither capacity nor opportunity nor freedom, even if we had inclination, for an openness commensurate with a love which was responding to and sharing in a love for all men. Further, love deals with neither structures nor statistics. Love as a palliative is, perhaps, something available to us but love as a totality is an impossibility.

From which it follows that love is incredible. For the unbearability and impossibility of love arise directly out of the intrinsic total demand and offer of love. The very existence of love is the affirmation that the human beings who love and are loved are of total and absolute worth. Therefore the very existence and truth of love is called in question.

But this is the very situation to which the gospel is addressed. The good news is that the kingdom of heaven is at hand and that there is the possibility of salvation from sin. This is to say that the loving energy of God to overcome contradictions with fulfilment is breaking in. Thus to abandon facing the dilemma which is so plain for the Christian faith and church at the present time or simply to abandon faith and church would be to despair of the absolute value of human being and becoming.

But if we are to face the dilemma in such a way as to recapture both the vision of the gospel and an appropriate practice and response we must probe as deeply as possible into the mutual interrelationships which can and should exist between understanding Christian identity and understanding human identity.

Here I would suggest that two very useful tools for our investigation and for the provocation for our insight lie in the concepts of *relationship* and *community* and their connection with our understanding of what it is to be a human person. It is clear that there are immense cultural and ideological differences in the understanding of what it is to be a 'person', what it is to be an 'individual', how being a person or an individual is related to being a member of a community or of society, and so on. Indeed the very way of stating the problems and possibilities involved in this area will be different in different languages and cultures, so that the very shape of the problems and possibilities will be seen and felt differently. Developing sensitivity to our own partialities and limitations here is a necessity for development in the sort of self-awareness and open exploration which is required if we are to be set free from tribalisms and parochialisms which end up in dehumanizing ways of being human.

However, I believe that a sufficiently open formation for furthering an exploration of the relationship between Christian identity and human identity can be found in the suggestion that *men and women are that which their relationships enable them to become*. This formulation is valuable because it reflects a certain convergence between, on the one hand, insights and hopes characteristic of Christian believing (arising from biblical pictures and traditional reflection) and, on the other, emphases and needs very widely recognized in current understandings of life, its forms and its demands. It is, moreover, not a definition of what it is to be human. Rather it can serve as a generator of investigations of what is involved and as a provocation for developing indications for and criteria about what is humanizing and what is dehumanizing. This is possible because the formulation is itself open and dynamic. All the terms in it have meanings as they stand but the final meaning which they can come to have depends on the interactions between them. Thus the formulation indicates that to be human is a process – indeed, that to be human is to be discovering what it is to be human and to be making or marring this process in the course of being part of it. It further leaves totally open the question of how far relationships can extend. The process is not necessarily confined to mutual relationships between men and women. They may be open to God, to a whole range of possibilities involving Transcendence in the midst. They also involve interactions with the non-human and non-personal environment. But the emphasis is on the effects and possibilities of relational interaction. Being and becoming human is basically a relational matter.

Such an understanding is wholly appropriate to the vision, faith or gospel about human beings which I have outlined earlier in this chapter as coming from the Christian insights which are found to be so contradicted in Christian practice. God is seen as giving himself for and in relationships and community which overcome what is destructive and build up the possibilities of creation and fulfilment. A Giver whose primary gift is the giving of himself as and for enabling love is clearly wholly committed to relationships both as method and as end of his existence and activity. (The final chapters are an attempt to develop this further in relation to the Christian symbols of the kingdom of God and the Trinity.) A relational formulation about human identity is, therefore, very appropriate from a Christian point of view. It is also appropriate to current understandings of the nature of reality within which and out of which we live. It is, further, appropriate to much current analysis of those factors and pressures which operate to distort our being and becoming human, including analysis which shows up Christian attitudes and structures as part of these distortions. (This last point is illustrated at some length in the immediately following chapters.)

As to current understandings of the nature of reality, we find that from many disciplines and sciences we are invited more and more to think of reality in terms of relationships and interacting systems. Thus physics develops through formulae dealing with interactional events rather than with concrete or discrete objects. The biological sciences have pioneered ways of understanding living organisms as systems made up of sub-systems and related systematically to their wider environments. Out of this biological understanding of the interrelationships between living systems there has developed a whole range of systems-thinking which has many applications in cybernetics, in engineering and communications, in the behavioural sciences and in the understanding of the behaviour of institutions. Basically all this depends on concepts of relationship and of feed-back effects between that which is interrelated. It is clear also that both psychological and sociological ways of studying human and social realities are much concerned with relationships. Finally, growing awareness of environmental problems has helped us to see how we are all part of ecological sub-systems which are related together in one global ecosystem. Life is indeed seen to be a vast, complex and yet closely interwoven bundle of relationships. These interrelationships are becoming clearer but we have not yet developed the new understandings and responses which this network of relationships requires. None the less the basic importance of a relational understanding is clear. We have a very clear convergence here between traditional Christian insights (whose implications have likewise been by no means responded to or lived up to) and current ways of thinking which we are being forced to adopt. It may be, therefore, that we have here a fruitful way into developing a useful and illuminating dialectic between an understanding of Christian identity and our hopes for human identity and a dialectic which may deepen and clarify our practical understanding of both.

Further, we are now alerted, as never before, to the immense effects on human living, both individual and corporate, of social, economic and political relationships. We shall consider this further from the next chapter onwards as we turn to consider the insights of Marx and Marxism. But we can draw attention at this point to the revolution in our awareness which has come about through the increasing understanding of the ideological, social and cultural factors which are at work on both the behaviour and the thought of human beings. Once again relational and systematic factors become of central importance, even if argument is still possible and necessary about how decisive and determinative these factors are. The effect of this shift of our awareness on personal faith, ethics and behaviour seems to be something which the vast majority of Christians find singularly difficult to recognize, let alone to face up to. Thus we are frequently confronted with Christian talk of love and salvation which is so moralistic and individualistic and so blind to the effects of structures and institutions for violence and dehumanization that the very gospel of love is called into question. This is a main source of Christian institutions, activities and behaviour constituting the contradiction of Christianity so it will be a major subject for our continuing investigation. At the moment, however, I am simply pointing to the convergence of Christian insights and of current understandings of natural and social reality on the sphere of relationships.

If we take these structural and relational aspects of our reality into account in our preliminary consideration of the connection between Christian identity and human identity, then I think we can provisionally argue that the promise of human identity is the possibility of relationships at all levels that will permit the full development of that community and communion whose possibilities can be glimpsed in fully face-to-face relationships and in loving between human persons. The threat to human identity lies in the evident fact that relationships at all levels operate with great ambiguity and that relationships between the different levels, most notably between the personal face-to-face and the more extended social, political and economic, operate in conflicting ways that threaten to be totally destructive.

If, then, men and women are that which their relationships enable them to become and we have no community which permits and promotes relationships tending to the mutual fulfilment of all, what fulfilling future can there be? Moreover what prospects are there now for human becoming, hoping and enjoying? How are we to face the contradictions between the glimpses of love, relationships and community on the one hand and, on the other, the realities which suggest so powerfully that love is unbearable, incredible and impossible?

It is the bearing of the proclaimed albeit contradicted Christian gospel and vision of love upon these conflicts and contradictions of human being and becoming which I wish to continue to examine. So we shall be continuing that search for Transcendence in the midst which will enable us to submit our fantasies and distortions to the realities of the vision of Human Being in and through these conflicts. Thus the next move is to proceed to some consideration of the alleged causes of man's inhumanity to man. What are the sources of our contradiction?

3

Obstacles to being human – concerning Marx, history and sin

I am attempting to explore the dilemmas and contradictions which face me as a Christian and as a human being. The first dilemma arises from the evident contradiction of Christianity. The second dilemma arises from the apparent contradiction of love. It is necessary, therefore, to look further into our human contradictions. Indeed, it would seem likely that to find appropriate understandings and practices here is essential both to any continuing Christian discipleship and to any hopeful and realistic pursuit of being human. If we are anxious not to deny or neglect the extent of the promises and possibilities involved in being human then we are obliged not to underestimate the threats which face our being and becoming human.

Clearly, then, a central question for anyone who cares about being human or who dares to have any hopes about being human is 'Why are men and women so contradicted and so contradictory?' This is a central question for anyone who wants to follow up the hint or possibility that love might be love. This seems all the more necessary as very much in our current patterns and fashions of living seems clearly to abandon the intimations of love. One symptom of this condition of ours and example of our current denial of love is the promotion and commendation of pornography, obscenity and sadism. No doubt the pathologies and cruelties of moralism, repression and self-righteousness in the field of so-called sexual morality are strong contributory causes to the unloving and unlovely disorder in this area. The history of Christian attitudes to human sexuality is certainly one more source for establishing the contradiction of Christianity. But the present cult of the removal of all limits and all privacy in this vital area of humanity and personality together with the claim that this is done in the name of freedom clearly presents and represents a total rejection of love. The idea that love, in its glory and in its costliness, reflects the depths and possibilities of what it is to be human is contemptuously flouted or ignored. All reverence for human loving is gone, perhaps because all hope is gone. There is no hope of love coming to any reality or fulfilment. This same total rejection of love as a realistic possibility is to be seen in the widespread use of torture and in the increasing readiness to resort to acts of random terrorism. Perhaps, too, we have become so weak in our expectations either of love or of hope that we cannot face the possible existence of sheer wickedness, that is to say of deliberate delight in, and choice of, that which is destructive and dehumanizing. In any case, it is clear that we are faced with this central question of why men and women are so contradicted and so contradictory.

The general pressure to ask this question can be seen to include at least three strands. First, any claim to or proclamation of a Vision has to face the question 'Why the falling short ?', or to be condemned as mere fantasy, escapism or indulgence. (We may contrast the use of drugs for so-called 'transcendent experience' which once again denies any ultimate reality to love, for there is a withdrawal from the field of relationships where love is made or marred.) To refuse to face this question would be a direct denial of Christianity where the Transcendence in the midst is believed above all to be concerned with love.

Secondly, the historical vehicle and source of the Christian vision is constantly contradicting its own vision. Christians and Christian churches are sources of the contradiction of Christianity. This may be a special case of human contradictoriness. In view of the very nature of the Christian vision and gospel perhaps this is the worst case of human contradictoriness. It may therefore be in some sense a test case. But is it a unique case or rather a representative case of the general condition ? Human hope may lie not in explaining away the contradiction or denying its existence but in being saved from it and in it. (This is more fully explored in chapter 5 under the title of 'The Hopefulness of Solidarity in Sin'.) Thirdly, we have a very powerful diagnosis of, and challenge to, human contradictions active among us. It is a diagnosis and challenge which has taken on a new lease of life as our century proceeds and is very active in the Third World. It has also been espoused by deeply committed and anguished Christians in Latin America and in some parts of South-East Asia. I refer, of course, to Marxism or to what I would prefer to call Marxian diagnoses and intuitions.

I realize that my initial difficulty about the term 'Marxism' places myself and my argument in a difficult and probably non-acceptable position vis-à-vis 'true' Marxists. It may be, however, that dialogue is not impossible as Marxists seem now to be becoming almost as pluralistic in their interpretations and approaches as are Christians. In this there may be much ground for hope. Certainly Marxists are no strangers to the idea that contradictions have to be confronted. However, I prefer to express my concern with and interest in 'Marxian diagnoses and intuitions' because I cannot see sufficient grounds for the Marxist claim to be scientific and I see as one more terrible threat to humanity any Marxist claim to be total as an explanation of human reality. None the less I believe that the Marxian diagnoses and intuitions about certain central features and forces of present social reality are the most appropriate, challenging and creative that are available to us. On the subject of obstacles to being human they have to be taken absolutely seriously. I refuse to believe however that they are to be taken absolutely, that is, as declaring and defining a total diagnosis and definition of reality. None the less it is my thesis that the issue of how the Marxist critique, challenge and programme is to be evaluated and responded to is a central critical issue in our concern for being human and becoming human, for the freedom and the future of man, and for the authenticity of Christian faith and gospel. This I hold because the Marxist critique seems to be the most powerful pointer to our sharpest present human contradictions and sources of inhumanity.

To develop this thesis I must start from a brief summary of what I understand to be the main thrust of Marx's critique of the development of society. If one can be so foolish as to summarize the gospel one can also presumably dare to summarize the main thrust of Marxism. There are equal possibilities of disagreement and refutation but broad understandings must be risked in order to assess practical possibilities and consequences and to get a picture of understandings of reality. Clearly if we are to have any grounded understanding of what is wrong in the human condition and what may be expected of being human we must have some grounded and articulated view of what sort of reality we are part of. To reject 'ultimate' or overall questions as meaningless is already to despair of being human.

I understand Marx to have formulated a theory of human and social reality which he believed to be deducible from a systematic survey of history and which gives us the opportunity of responding to historical happenings in such a way as to assist in their positive development.

This has the following main features.

1. Members of all human societies (other than the most primitive) fall into two categories – the ruling class and the subject class or classes.

2. The dominance of the ruling class is explained by their control of the means of economic production. This dominance is consolidated politically by the ruling class's control over military force and over the production of ideas.

3. The ruling class and the subject classes are in conflict. The developments in this conflict are influenced primarily by technological changes effecting the methods and means of production.

4. Modern capitalist societies make the class conflict clearer and clearer because they promote a polarization of wealth and power over against poverty and dependence.

5. The class struggle will end with the victory of the working class and out of this will emerge a classless society.

The power and relevance of the insights systematized in and expressed through this theory are not automatically vitiated by the theory as a whole being less than satisfactory (for example, difficulty about the rise of the feudal ruling class) or less total than it claims. The claim to totality is a typical piece of human arrogance in a Western tribal form. Why should it be assumed that a philosophy emerging from Western philosophical traditions and a technology developed in the West and exported and exploited by the West should provide *the* clue to history and the moving force of history? To this point we shall have to return in order to consider it further not only with regard to Marxism but also with regard to Western Christian views, including their historicizing of the Bible. I simply draw attention to it now to set on one side the argument that Marxist insights can be ignored just because they are promoted and pursued within the falsifying and hubristic context of a claim to total explanation, a claim arising out of a strictly limited perspective.

Similarly, the fact that Marx was enough of a Western optimist about progress (and possibly enough of an atheistic biblicist) to round off his theory with a messianic myth about the working class and a classless society and so turn his social criticism into a secular gospel, does not undermine the validity of his critical insights into present social reality. Of course, it has effects on the programmes suggested for responding to the criticized and critical situations and to this again we shall have to return. But for the moment I wish to concentrate as sharply and forcefully as possible on the validity of the Marxist judgment *upon* society, whatever may be the weakness or inherent dangers of the Marxist gospel *for* society. Indeed, I would sum up the thesis which I am trying to put forward at this stage in my argument and exploration by stating my conviction that unless we face up to the Marxist judgment *on* society we shall have no authentic or legitimately credible gospel for human beings *in* society.

This is because Marx has drawn our attention in a particularly compelling and articulated way to three features of life in society which Christians in common with many others in Western society have tended to ignore or reject, viz.: Exploitation: Conflict: Control in the production and understanding of ideas. He has further pointed out that these three features are functions of, that is to say, decisively influenced by, the class of those in power.

As, for the greater part of its history so far, Christianity has in the main been effectively identified with those in power (unlike Jesus), this revelation of Marx has a devastating effect on the position of Christian faith and church as a source of both gospel and mission. It is peculiarly relevant to an exercise in white bourgeois theology. My belief, however, is that its relevance is liberating and not destructive – but only if faced rather than denied or ignored.

These notions of ruling class, class conflict, class exploitation and class ideology are, of course, bitterly contested and I do not have the technical expertise to subject them to detailed analysis and criticism. I can only record my judgment that they record and reflect an intuition – an insight into the way social reality functions – which tells me something about myself and those with whom I enjoy the closest 'we-feeling'. This is something which I recognize, once it has been pointed out, as true. To use my religious vocabulary – Marxism convicts me of sin. ('*Thou* art the man.') And it is the conviction of sin which is the beginning of the possibility of repentance and of discovering the gospel.

The most immediately telling point, that which convicts me as under judgment, is that about ideology, that is to say, the claim that the way we understand reality is a function of our class interests and that the dominating class succeeds, until effectively challenged, in imposing that set of ideas and understandings which is in accordance with its own interests. This seems to me to be something which, once it is pointed out and perceived, is so obvious as to be both undeniable and irrefutable. It is a form of self-awareness which changes one's way of seeing things. As I hope the subsequent development of my investigations will show, I do not understand the claim about ideology in a wholly deterministic sense. An overall pattern, configuration or trend does not necessarily determine the shape or behaviour of every single one of its parts. Nor do I hold that there is or can emerge a class or group which is 'ideologically pure', i.e., whose way of looking at things is 'the truth'. This is why I insist on treating the exposure of ideological influence as an intuition rather than a scientifically established, precise and wholly generalizable description. Rather it shows me a very widespread feature of and influence on the thoughts and behaviour of myself, my fellows and, as far as I can see, on human beings as a whole. It is because I see this influence at work wherever I turn and constantly find an ideological analysis illuminating about the realities being faced in any particular problem that I term the insight 'undeniable and irrefutable'.

It is, of course denied because of its disturbing effects and because of the radical repentance it requires if true. In this it is very like the judgment of God (see further later and especially chapters 5 and 8). A crucial question thus arises whether any resource or grace is available to promote such repentance or whether nothing can be done except by the dictatorship of the proletariat and counter-repression, allegedly *en route* for general (classless) liberty. However, the fact that an insight makes apparently impossible demands is no evidence that it is false. And, as I say, it seems to me to be plainly true and something I recognize in myself.

Indications of the ubiquity of this ideological element can, for example, be detected by simple inspection of or reflection on many items reported in the newspapers and on the fashion in which they are reported or commented on. The lectures which form the basis of this present book were being prepared and delivered at the time of the miners' strike and the general election to which it led in March 1974. A particular headline which I then noted, in *The Daily Telegraph* on 5 January 1974, said, 'Miners Caught in Socialist Trap'. This was hardly the way the situation was described in such left-wing papers as there are. Nor did it seem consistent with the way interviewed miners or their leaders understood the situation. An analysis of the correspondence columns of different papers over the whole period of both the 1974 election campaigns also provided abundant evidence for the differing ways in which the same 'reality' is to be 'really' understood. Towards the end of 1974 a headline in one paper referred to the 'restraint' indicated by the government's decision to defer half of a recommended rise to senior judges, civil servants and services personnel. If this is compared with comments made from other quarters the influence of the 'we' from whose point of view the judgment is made becomes obvious.

Further evocative examples can be found by studying the pronouncements of many 'leading people', including bishops, about 'national unity', 'the common interest' and 'the need for consensus'. They nearly always imply the maximum preservation of the status quo and assume that what we now have is, at least very nearly, the proper norm of 'the nation's need' and will best meet the legitimate needs of citizens. On the 'Law and Order' issue it was interesting for me personally to compare the reported reasons given for not renewing local authority support to the Notting Hill Law Centre with the way the situation was understood by persons involved, directly or at secondhand, with the work of that Centre and its role in the neighbourhood. Or, again, it may or may not be significant that in an article published in *The Times* on Christmas Eve 1973, Mr Enoch Powell chose to begin by referring to all those Christmas sermons which 'must fain inform us that he was born in a stable among the cattle because the rich and the heartless had left "no room at the inn" for Mary and Joseph'. As far as I can judge there is a strong case for Mr Powell's exegetical destruction of the myth of the stable and no room at the inn. It appears likely, however, that his concern in publishing this piece of New Testament scholarship was not simply for the historic truth about the birth of Jesus. Finally, as a sort of barometric indication of the way in which we tend to be caught, naturally, in the centre of our own particular class and cultural per-spectives I would suggest some self-examination about one's feeling-reactions to TV interviews of people involved in economic, political or industrial crises. For myself, I find that I can often detect a difference and even a conflict between the critical reflection I am attempting to make about what is actually being said and the way I feel about who is saying it. For example, even when I intellectually reject what is being said by a politician or minister, as so many of them have clearly been to grammar school and university like myself they remain among the 'us'. On the other hand, even when I accept what is being said by a trade union official he tends to remain one of 'them'.

Thus from all sides and from within ourselves we are increasingly alerted to the limitations of class or of some form of 'tribalism' which takes our own 'we-group' as the norm and which attempts to insist that this norm of 'ours' is the general and decisive one which should have the dominance. Hence I take this 'ideological' point first from the Marxist critique because it is crucial, first, to understanding the other points. From whose point of view is one assessing and responding to a situation? Can we be saved from, while still in, our tribalism? Secondly it questions very sharply the possibility of a universal being human or of a universal gospel. Are we trapped in our relativities and partialities and at the mercy of nothing but a process of conflict? Here again it is possible to see the absolute cruciality of the question of the possibility of 'Transcendence in the midst'. We may transpose to our context the cry of Paul (Rom. 7.24), 'Who shall deliver us from the body of this death ?' This seems to me all the more necessary a question as the myth of the messianic class leading to a classless utopia seems a delusion quite unsupported by history, experience or psychology. (But this last point is to anticipate.)

The crucial point at the moment is the validity of the insight that, both at the level of society and politics, our judgments tend to be a function of our own interests, at least in the case of the dominating classes, and that these judgments are taken as universal not only by the dominating classes but also by those whom they dominate, as long as that domination is undisturbed. This leads on to the next point that what chiefly disturbs this predominance of a ruling class understanding is the growth of awareness about the realities of exploitation, that is, the development of a corresponding class consciousness. This is the awareness that a limited number of people live at the disproportionate expense of the majority. Awareness of this has developed with general force over the last century and with accelerating speed over say, the last thirty years with the break-up of the former Western colonial empires.

It should be noted that there is a close connection between a growing awareness of the reality of exploitation and a developing understanding of human freedom and responsibility. To be able to point to exploitation as a feature of present human societies and of the world situation as a whole we must also hold that human social reality is a human construct and not just a reflection of some ordered reality which has its divisions and relationships built in by something like divine fiat or law. Justice then shifts from being a matter of attempting to see that everyone receives what is due according to their status and position in the ordered hierarchy, with the acceptance of vast differences between these 'dues', to a matter of a concern for equality – in participation, in consumption and in enjoyment.

It may well be held that the situation adumbrated and hoped for in the famous 'from each according to his ability and to each according to his need' is a noble but romantic idea incapable of attainment. It is also clear that there are immense practical difficulties and obscurities in the notion of 'equality'. But neither the difficulties inherent here nor even the present or foreseeable impossibility of achievement remove the truth lying in the diagnosis, unless we give up all attempt to relate together love and being human. For this notion of an equality to be striven for, linked with the notion of freedom and responsibility in and for human social structures, is clearly wholly consistent with, if not required by, what I have cited as the insight of love, namely, that no one can be fully human until everyone is fully human. This requires equality and mutuality of participation, use and enjoyment. A corresponding insight to this is that everyone is as human as everyone else – an insight which is persistently denied by all forms of exploitation and tribalism. Thus the discovery by peoples, classes and races who have hitherto been dependent and made use of for the power, consumption and enjoyment of a limited class of their fellows that they are oppressed and exploited is an essential step in their discovery of their true humanness. (It does *not* constitute or complete the humanness.) Whatever turbulence and difficulties, indeed violence and destruction, this may cause or threaten to cause, it seems clear that any vision and gospel of love must face this reality of exploitation and the basic humanness of the revolt against it. It is a necessary stage in the practical discovery of a truly common humanity.

Nor does it seem possible to mitigate the sharpness of this issue of exploitation by the claim that developed industrial society has moved into a post-ideological stage when power is widely diffused and exploitation is sufficiently muted by a form of social redistribution. Exploitation remains a reality both within our own society and because of the way in which the world economic system still operates. Within our own society, whatever may be the effects of taxation, inflation and the provision of public services upon the redistribution of wealth, it is easy to show that power, the ownership of wealth and the opportunities for gaining access to power and wealth still remain concentrated in the hands of a very largely self-perpetuating minority.[1] It is, in any case, obvious that access to educational opportunities which in turn provide access to more influential or better paid employment and access to health facilities, for example, are very unevenly distributed. In a period when economic growth is becoming restricted and the patterns of consumption will have to change, questions of equality and justice in distribution are clearly going to become more pressing. We shall find more and more pressing the question about who pays what costs and who gets what benefits. Thus the whole structure of rewards, status and power as it has grown up in our society is bound to become more and more in question. There will be no opportunity to continue with the myth that as society as a whole grows richer so everyone becomes more

[1] The type of arguments and sets of statistics which can be marshalled here can be found e.g. in the essay by J. Westergaard ,'Sociology: the Myth of Classlessness', in *Ideology in Social Science*, ed. R. Blackburn, Collins (Fontana) 1972, pp. 119 ff., or in the article by Martin Meacher, 'The Coming Class Struggle', in *The New Statesman*, 4 January 1974.

equal and class is naturally eroded. The question of power, of exploitation and of what can constitute a common social purpose will have to be faced.

The question about exploitation is also made both more complex and more urgent by the increasing awareness in the so-called Third World countries of the way in which their economies have been dependent on and exploited by the hitherto rich countries and also by the way in which these countries are now organizing to counter-attack. There are numerous difficulties arising out of the complex effects on the poor of the developed countries arising from the Third World resisting exploitation by the rich countries. There are also great problems about the ruling classes in the Third World countries themselves. Further it now seems likely that the successful tactics of the oil-producing countries are producing a Fourth World of countries being pushed into even deeper impoverishment. But all this simply underlines the reality of exploitation, especially as sharply highlighted by Marxist theory, and makes it clear that here we have a main human fact and challenge of our time, a challenge moreover which is put before us not only by Marxism but also by the gospel.

Since this is so, it is equally clear that a basic factor in our human situation is that of conflict, a conflict between those who have ignored or denied the equal humanness of some men and women and those who are becoming conscious that their humanness has been so ignored and exploited. Moreover this conflict cannot be clamped down or side-stepped by appeals to the sanctity or, indeed, the necessity of sacrifices and poverty. It seems clear that there is an essential role for sacrifice and for a certain poverty in any really hopeful becoming human or in any creative living with the problems, conflicts and limitations of our lives but at this level of the argument it can be dangerously irrelevant and exploitive to bring in the reference. I shall return to this theme, especially in chapter 8. Meanwhile it must be made clear that to demand sacrifices where they are not matched in one's own style of life is one more form of oppression and exploitation, an exaction compounded with hypocrisy. To offer sacrifice and poverty is another matter. But this is a direct challenge to us, not a challenge which we can issue to others. It is also a challenge which has to be faced alongside, and perhaps as part of, the issues of oppression and exploitation within our own society and in the world at large. It is certainly clear that the struggle against oppression in society and in history cannot but involve conflict.

Thus it seems to me that we derive from Marxist theory, treated as a source of veridical intuitions, an understanding that social reality involves exploitation, conflict and a control over the production of ideas, including our ideas of what is real, just, and appropriate to various classes of human beings.

Do we therefore conclude that the total cause of man's inhumanity to man is oppression (distorting both oppressors and oppressed and accounting for all their various malformations of themselves and of one another) and, that the only obstacle to being and becoming human is constituted by the social structures of class and exploitation with their roots in economic power? And so do we further hold that our hopes for what is involved in being and becoming human lie in the class struggle now and in the emergence, via the dictatorship of the proletariat, of the classless society?

I have already indicated that I believe that the diagnosis of Marxism has to be taken absolutely seriously while the claim to absoluteness – of diagnosis, of description and of hope – has to be rejected. To locate the cause of man's contradictions of himself solely in oppression and the obstacles to overcoming these contradictions in social and economic structures seems to be a dangerously insufficient account of what is involved both in the human dilemma and in the human possibility, while the hope and assurance of a future solution and resolution through the class struggle to a classless society seems to be quite unrealistic and groundless.

There is a deep error here about the nature of human reality and of the relationships and possibilities which are involved in and open to human beings. One chief aspect of the error is to confine man to history. The other is to be blind to the complexities of sin. The effect of this compound mistake is an inevitable tendency to a limiting totalitarianism which cannot but add to the dehumanizing forces at work in history and in human relationships.

But I must here repeat my conviction already expressed that it is not possible to proceed with the critique of Marxism which these considerations require unless the Marxist critique of society and especially of Western society, and, within that, especially of the role and behaviour of the Christian church in society is, at the same time, fully faced. This is because that Marxist critique reveals to us aspects of the reality of our existence which demand judgment and repentance – a judgment and a repentance which is wholly consistent with the demands and possibilities of Christian faith and love.

I am quite clear that I cannot myself adequately perform the task to which I am here pointing. I must however attempt to assist its development by identifying and clarifying one or two contributions which will help in embarking on it. As with all truly human and truly Christian tasks, its nature can be fully discovered only as we commit ourselves to it. So my method now will be to explore the interrelation between the Marxist judgment upon society and the Marxist errors of putting too much weight on history and too little weight on sin by considering the biblical and prophetic judgments upon society expressed with reference to the treatment and fate of the poor. I believe that once again there is a convergence to be perceived between biblical and Christian insights and those developed in another strand of human and historical experience and reflection. The Marxist criticism of our society converges at some important points with the biblical and prophetic judgment which is proclaimed upon the treatment of the poor and the excluded.

4

Judgment from the poor and the excluded

According to Marxism the reality of human being and becoming has so far been characterized by the division of mankind into two main classes, the exploited and the exploiters. Until the oppressed, who are the vast majority and constitute the primary producers and workers, become aware of their oppression and fight for their liberation against the class of their oppressors, mankind cannot begin to be freed from all that distorts and denies the human possibilities. The liberation of human becoming lies, therefore, through the class conflict and the dictatorship of the masses which will lead on to the mutual interdependence and freedom of the classless society. Abolish class and thereby get rid of exploitation. This will remove both the contradictions and the contradictoriness of human beings.

Here we have a realistic description of the way the majority of our societies operate and of the way the present world economy operates. The few live richly at the expense of the many. The majority of these many live, moreover, not just rather more badly than those in power but very badly indeed, in conditions which increasingly threaten their basic humanity, let alone its flowering and fulfilment. Secondly, *all* of these many lack the opportunity to have any control over what life asks of them or gives to them. Being exploited and being dominated go together. Hence to find a way of fighting all this is to find a way of discovering, asserting and developing one's very humanity.

With this combination of realism about the way the structures of the world actually work and the offering of a hope and response which is practically graspable for the masses within the severe limitations which these structures impose, it is not surprising that an increasing number of Christians see this Marxist approach as the focus within current realities for a belief in, and response to, the kingdom of God as manifested by Jesus. Here is the working-out of Transcendence in the midst and of God become man.

There are strong pressures which reinforce the readiness to embrace and develop this convergence between Marxist insights and Christian faith. On the one hand Christians who become aware of the extent of the identification of the church with the privileged status quo suffer a strong sense of guilt and of shock. They are moved and disturbed by this discovery of the contradiction of Christianity. The Marxist analysis reinforces the condemnation which these awakened Christians feel that they and their church both need and deserve, while at the same time a positive way forward is indicated. Something can be done to pass beyond this condemnation. On the other hand many Christians who turn to Marxism are excited by the way in which men and women among the poor and the oppressed discover themselves and find hope in being themselves as they begin to take on their historical role according to this doctrine and analysis. If you discover that you can organize and work together to achieve something for yourself then you also discover that you are indeed a self. And this discovery can be made through and in the solidarity and purposiveness of the struggle whether or not the struggle leads to immediate achievement. Thus Christians have come to see this discovery by the poor and the oppressed that they can have a part, a meaning, and a hope in the shaping of their own lives, as real foretastes or sacraments of the kingdom of God. This kingdom represents the final power for the final fulfilment of men and women, a power which is fighting with all that seeks to overcome or to deny it. It has always been believed that the kingdom is known through various experiences of 'real presence' in the midst of the things which contradict or ignore it. When men and women discover the possibilities of their humanity in the midst of so much that contradicts or ignores it, are they not receiving realistic sacraments of the kingdom? Moreover these real signs are received much more within the realities of actual human situations than often seems to be the case with the more formal and ritualized sacraments of the churches.

There are, therefore, positive as well as negative pressures which encourage the discovery of a convergence and a collaboration between Marxists and Christians. These are further strengthened by the strong strand of anti-transcendentalism which exists in much modern Christian and theological thought. The struggle against oppression seems to be a particularly appropriate secular and historical form for the fight against sin and for the realization of salvation which is also liberation. I shall hope to show that anti-transcendentalism is a mistake and a denial of the Christian gospel and of human possibilities. But it must be admitted that what Guttierez and others have pointed to as the luxuries of transcendentalism, personalism and existentialism have constituted another contributory source of the contradiction of Christianity. Alleged devotion to the values of the transcendental, the personal or the existential has been expressed in ways which have encouraged and justified forms of religious practice which have tried to keep outside the realities of that social struggle and suffering which is the stuff of so much human living. In this these values have been made use of in anti-historical and so in anti-incarnational ways. Hence a reaction towards forms of secular involvement is understandable. It also fits in with the reactions to the sense of guilt and of shock to which I have already referred. Over against the luxury of transcendentalism we must set the involvement of struggle.

Finally, the whole approach is reinforced in a most powerful way by the echoes in it of the prophetic and biblical concern for the poor. This I shall be discussing at greater length later in this chapter but it clearly provides a very strong prima facie case for taking very seriously the deeply practical concern for the lot of the poor and the oppressed in society which is so strong a motivating force in Marxism. I should like to give a fairly extensive quotation from an important example of this type of approach which has recently become reasonably well-known in this country. I regard the quotation as important because it comes from a considered and singularly well-documented work and sets out the essential features of the argument and understanding so clearly. I also think that it well indicates some of the points which give rise to questioning and give grounds for legitimate disquiet. The quotation comes from the work of Gustavo Guttierez already referred to. Speaking of the Exodus, he says:

> By working, transforming the world, breaking out of servitude, building a just society, and assuming his destiny in history man forges himself. In Egypt, work is alienated and, far from building a just society, contributes rather to increasing injustice and to widening the gap between exploiters and exploited.
>
> To dominate the earth as Genesis prescribed, to continue creation, is worth nothing if it is not done for the good of man, if it does not contribute to his liberation, in solidarity with all, in history. The liberating initiative of Yahweh responds to this need by stirring up Moses' vocation. Only the mediation of this self-creation – first revealed by the liberation from Egypt – allows us to rise above poetic expressions and general categories and to understand in a profound and synthesizing way the relationship between creation and salvation so vigorously proclaimed by the Bible.

The Exodus experience is paradigmatic. It remains vital and contemporary due to similar historical experiences which the People of
God undergo. As Neher writes, it is characterized 'by the twofold sign
of the overriding will of God and the free and conscious consent of
men'. And it structures our faith in the gift of the Father's love. In
Christ and through the Spirit, men are becoming one in the very heart
of history, as they confront and struggle against all that divides and
opposes them. But the true agents of this quest for unity are those who
today are oppressed (economically, politically, culturally) and struggle
to become free. Salvation – totally and freely given by God, the communion of men with God and among themselves – is the inner force and
the fullness of this movement of man's self generation which was
initiated by the work of creation..

Consequently, when we assert that man fulfills himself by continuing
the work of creation by means of his labor, we are saying that he places
himself, by this very fact, within an all-embracing salvific process. To
work, to transform this world, is to become a man and to build the
human community; it is also to save. Likewise, to struggle against
misery and exploitation and to build a just society is already to be part
of the saving action, which is moving towards its complete fulfillment.
All this means that building the temporal city is not simply a stage of
'humanization' or 'pre-evangelization' as was held in theology up until
a few years ago. Rather it is to become part of a saving process which
embraces the whole of man and all human history.[1]

Now, while wanting to hold firmly to the revealing truth of the
Marxist judgment upon us and upon our historical situation to which I
have been drawing attention and which I shall develop further later, I
see several grounds on which features of this passage must be drastically
questioned.

These questions include the following and it is not at all clear to me
that the argument and approach as a whole provides any adequate or
hopeful answer to them. Firstly, we are told: 'By working, transforming
the world, breaking out of servitude, building a just society, and assuming
his destiny in history man forges himself.' Later this is repeated and
developed in the form: 'To work, to transform this world, is to become
a man and to build the human community; it is also to save.' We must
ask, it seems to me, what hope is this and what hope is there of this?
When we combine these words with the reference about 'To dominate
the earth as Genesis prescribed . . .' we seem to be in the atmosphere of
the nineteenth-century Western confidence in progress and the insistence of the Protestant ethic on the supreme value and triumph of
work rather than in the more pessimistic climate of the last quarter of
the twentieth century. Certainly the confident assertion 'it is also to

[1] *A Theology of Liberation*, pp. 159 f.

save' seems to require support which is not obviously available from history, from nature or from the Bible.

This particular question extends to doubts about the claims made for man and about what it is claimed he can achieve, apparently by his efforts *alone*. Thus '*only* (my italics) the mediation of this self-creation ... allows us . . . to understand . . . the relationship between creation and salvation', as if creation endowed man with all the necessary potentialities for salvation. One's suspicion of over-optimism and unreality here is strengthened by two other statements contained in the quotation. First, 'In Christ and through the Spirit, men are becoming one. . . .' It seems necessary to be specific about which men where. It is quite possible that this unity is experienced by a mere handful of travelled intellectuals, that struggles are as likely to lead to fragmention as to unity and that the 'becoming one in the very heart of history' is the perception of a few bourgeois intellectuals. Secondly, the quotation within my quotation which declares that the Exodus experience was characterized by 'the twofold sign of the overriding will of God and the free and conscious consent of men' seems to be plainly false of Israel at least as portrayed in the biblical accounts. The history of the people of God seems to be concerned with a constant struggle between God and this people and with the constant need for God to overrule or overcome the way his people perverted their calling. This misrepresentation seems typical of the way the approach we are considering fails to give weight to a sufficiently deep notion of sin or to the biblical presentation of the evidence. This does not prove the approach false – only that we cannot legitimately use the Bible to support it.

This misrepresentation seems to persist even in the references to the poor, even though, as I shall shortly argue, the biblical presentation concerning the poor is a place where a most important convergence with Marxism occurs. Gutierrez writes: 'But the *true* (my italics) agents of this quest for unity are those who today are oppressed ... and struggle to become free.' The question that arises here is whether this messianic view of the oppressed is sustainable. There is also the question whether a simple division of mankind into 'true' agents of unity and of the salvation of God, i.e., the oppressed, and 'false' agents, i.e., oppressors, does justice to the complexities of human society and history or to the range of resources and possibilities involved in being human. I shall argue later that a dehumanizing rather than a liberating doctrine of man is lurking here.

It seems unlikely, therefore, that a solution to our problems and a resolution to our contradictions will be provided by syntheses of this type between Christian and Marxist insights. The difficulty of finding a way to proceed does not, however, invalidate the intuitions which have brought us this far. The revelations about the unjust and oppressive nature of our societies stand. The pressures which I have referred to as leading Christians to develop the convergences between Marxist and Christian insights reflect a great deal of what is real and urgent for any who care about the development and fulfilment of men and women. Further, poverty is clearly at the centre of our present human dilemma and challenge. For we are not only faced with the sufferings and demands of the poor but also with the rapidly accumulating evidence that the world cannot sustain our present forms of exploitation, affluence and richness. I want therefore to turn to a reconsideration of the biblical evidence concerning the poor. What convergence is there with the Marxist approach and what possible divergence is there? There can be no doubt that the poor and the oppressed are of particular significance for discussing the judgment of God upon society and so for seeing the offer of God to society.

As Gutierrez himself points out, especially in his chapter thirteen, there is much prophetic denunciation of the oppression and exploitation of the poor in a fashion which is both powerful and specific, that is, in a fashion which requires 'political' forms of repentance. Response requires changes in society. There is the well-known denunciation of Amos (2.6 f., NEB):

> I will grant them no reprieve,
> because they sell the innocent for silver
> and the destitute for a pair of shoes.
> They grind the heads of the poor into the earth
> and thrust the humble out of the way.

Elsewhere fraudulent commerce and exploitation are condemned along with hoarding of lands, dishonest courts, violence of the ruling classes, slavery, unjust taxes and unjust officials.

These prophetic denunications always relate to the judgment of God upon society. It is because this sort of behaviour is rife in the society that the day of the Lord will come as an occasion of judgment and destruction and not as some occasion of vindication. The Lord will not fight for his people. He will be against them. Thus the oppression and neglect of the poor throws into relief those features of society which are contrary to the will of God for his covenant people.

Similarly, it is by paying attention to those whom our societies leave poor or make poor that we can be alerted to those features of our social and political life which are under the judgment of God. That is to say that it is the condition and treatment of the poor which point most sharply to those practices of ours which contradict the gospel of love, according to which all human beings are as human as all others so that no human being can be fully human without all being fully human. Thus, the prophetic references to the lot of the poor certainly confirm the idea that it is from the poor that we are to receive discerning and creative judgment upon our society, and that this is not simply a matter of lack of charity, but of judgment upon the structures of our society as a whole. As an example of how this insight might be applied, consider the following sketch of some considerations about urban poverty.

Cities can be seen to concentrate the collective ills of the human condition and confront us with them. In particular, they provide concrete flesh-and-blood evidence at every turn of how the majority of men, women and children in the world belong to those classes who can best be described as the underprivileged, the dispossessed and the marginals.

That the dwellers in urban slums are 'underprivileged' is obvious. For every city has, at its business heart and in its select areas, large numbers of the privileged whose wealth and opportunities are obvious and are in stark contrast with the mass of the urban population. Thus the city brings into sharp focus what is true of the global situation of mankind, namely that some 15% of the world's population consume 85% of the world's production and that there is a very thin crust in poor countries and a thicker, but even so not very extensive, crust in richer countries of privileged consumers with access to services and opportunities either totally denied or very poorly available to the majority.

But the situation is worse than the mere contrast between rich and poor, privileged and underprivileged. Cities, especially in the Third World countries, are constantly sucking in the rural populations. The favellas, shanty-towns and areas of improvised shacks are full of those whom the maelstrom of economic pressure and economic change has dragged from the poverty of the countryside to the degradation of the city. Hence families who had a recognizable identity, role and share in a village community, however poor, disappear into the vastness and anonymity of the urban proletariat who belong nowhere and have no continuing pattern of life. Hence, once again, the city brings into focus all those pressures of modern economic, social and political life which take away the identities and human possibilities of so many and leave them dispossessed both of their roots and of their rights to contribute to their own destiny, with the barest of lives for the present and no apparent hope for the future.

The city also reflects the humanly destructive trends at work among us which drive numbers of people to the margins of our present society. The aspect of the functioning of our society which I am trying to draw attention to here is not quite the same as those pointed to by referring to the underprivileged and the dispossessed. The grossly underprivileged and the dispossessed are, of course, marginal in our society in the sense that they are left on the edge of the main activities of the society, those which produce and make use of its benefits, opportunities and goods. But by making a separate point about 'marginals' I wish to emphasize the ways in which our society is even more active in promoting human misery than my brief description of the previous two categories might indicate. (Of course, none of my three categories are precisely defined or exclusive of one another. I am attempting a sketch, not a precisely analytical chart.) Because, for example, of an interacting set of factors to do with the increasing cost of urban land, of providing urban services and maintaining urban accommodation, more and more people who cannot get out of cities or who find themselves forced into cities become 'marginal' in the sense indicated above. For example the old, those on fixed pensions, those who are handicapped by a physical disability, by being members of a one-parent family or by belonging to a so-called 'coloured' race are often driven below the poverty line. Thus poverty is manufactured, for groups such as these, by the dynamics of the operations of society.

It is for reasons such as these that it seems we must consider the poor as of central significance in our understanding of our society and of our way of life. The 'poor' here are all those whom society is effectively treating as less than human because they are being used (i.e. exploited) for the production of its enjoyments which they do not have, are being left outside the operation and benefits of society or are being positively driven outside what the more well-off and powerful take for granted. The way the poor are treated as less than human reveals the essentially dehumanizing trends at work throughout society. Thus the poor (in the extended sense to take in the marginals and the excluded and not just the physically grossly underprivileged) are not just *a* problem of society. There is focused in them, in their flesh and blood and their deprivations, *the* problem of society. It is in this sense that they are signs of the judgment of the kingdom.

Hence the poor and the marginals are not primarily objects of charity and compassion but rather subjects and agents of the judgment of God and pointing to the ways of the kingdom. This seems to be the conclusion which is required when one sees the compelling convergence between the humanly disturbing features of our present condition of which our cities provide one striking set of examples, and the prophetic announcement of judgment upon those who oppress the poor. Further, such a conclusion is not merely consistent with but required by the biblical portrayal of God as the Disturber.

Christian talk about God is usually particularly concerned with God as reconciler and with the possibilities of reconciliation in situations of conflict or alienation. Ultimately and basically this reflects a valid insight of faith. The kingdom of God is concerned with the reconciliation and fulfilment of all things. But how is the point and place to be reached where a mutual reconciliation which promotes and achieves mutual fulfilment becomes possible? Only by getting rid of those features of institutions and structures and those aspects and patterns of social and individual behaviour which promote conflict and make one man's fulfilment dependent on another's distortion or loss. Thus the way to reconciliation and fulfilment must be through conflict with evil and through much disturbance and even destruction of what many may regard as their fulfilment and hopes. A truly omniscient and overcoming love clearly cannot tolerate anything which prevents the free flow of love between all who exist both to love and be loved and so must work against all obstructions.

The struggle and conflict of love is a strong strand in the biblical portrayal of God's dealings with his people and with the nations. This strand has frequently been neglected by Christians of all traditions who have tended to prefer a complacent and self-centred interpretation of the divine calling, comfort and promise which is offered to them. Or else the call to be part of the fight against evil has been interpreted as justifying a self-righteous attack on, or domination over, those different from us who have been identified as the enemies of God. But these misunderstandings and abuses do not blot out the significant message that with love there goes wrath. God is against those who obstruct the ways of love. This is part of his love for all and of his energy for the eventual achievement of the wholeness of love. It is therefore, part of his love for those whom he is against.

We dare not and must not interpret any statement of this sort as implying that this conflict of God with men is a mere demonstration. The judgment and the wrath are real, for the love is real and the contradictions of love are real. As I have already stressed at the beginning of this exploration, there can be no smooth and comforting syntheses. If these things are to be overcome it is because of Transcendence in the midst which suffers them through to some healing outcome, not because of some remote Transcendence which allows them to be explained away. This is made finally clear by the fact that Jesus, who is the identification of God with man and the identification of man with God, reaches the climax of his personal mission through his passion, on the cross and by his death. If there is resurrection it is through human, historical and flesh-and-blood suffering and defeat. The resurrection is not restoration achieved by the divine waving of a cosmic fairy wand. It is the demonstration and the discovery that God himself enters the conflicts and suffers the contradictions.

We have, therefore, to take with the utmost seriousness the reality of God's controversy with his people.

> Hear ye, O mountains, the Lord's controversy, and ye enduring foundations of the earth: for the Lord hath a controversy with his people and he will plead with Israel (Micah 6.2).

> Hear the word of the Lord, ye children of Israel: for the Lord hath a controversy with the inhabitants of the land, because there is no truth, nor mercy, nor knowledge of God in the land (Hosea 4.1).

This controversy is because of a failure in religion which is reflected in a failure to care for justice, as the chapter from Micah in particular makes clear. Thus, as we are on our way to the kingdom, we must expect to encounter God as the Disturber in the interests of true reconciliation and of an ultimate peace which is in accordance with love. He is a Disturber of all that which stands in the way of developing towards a fully human society. Any serious reflection on what Marxist analysis has to point us to about oppression and on what the Bible has to say about the poor and about God's controversy with his people recalls us to the disturbing and basically revolutionary ways of this God. His concern is to overthrow what is contrary to the fulfilment of human beings in truth, mercy, justice and love. Because of the oppression, alienation and contradictions of which we are part we can have no grounds for looking for reconciliation without disturbance.

Does this mean that after all we must unreservedly endorse the view indicated by Gutierrez in the passage from which I quoted, where he writes: 'The true agents of this quest for unity are those who today are oppressed (economically, politically, culturally) and struggle to be free'? And do we equate the class struggle with the struggle for and of the kingdom of God? I do not think that the evidence either of the Bible or of human history and experience supports such an endorsement or equation.

Before I go on, in fear and trembling, to expand this crucial and critical point let me insert one further set of observations, which I also hold to be crucial. I am developing my argument by considering and criticizing a type of argument and exposition put forward by Christians in a number of contexts at present but especially in Latin America, and I am making particular use of the form of the argument developed by Fr Gutierrez. It will destroy the force of my argument if it is understood as being directed at Christians and Christian theologians in Latin America (as well as elsewhere) and criticizing them for identifying themselves with Marxists in some particular political struggles. I do not believe that I have either sufficient material for making, or sufficient right to make, any such criticism.

In any case I am quite clear that the decision about concrete forms of political and social involvement must be ultimately made by Christians in a particular situation, locality or country. I shall return to this point in my chapter on radical spirituality and radical politics. I do not regard it as a merely incidental point but as a central one for ecumenical Christian consideration. We have to wrestle together with the relationship between the necessary particularity of our commitments and the universality both of the Christian gospel and our Christian hope. I am trying to develop an experiment in white bourgeois English theology. This I intend as a contribution to the sort of critical and open, but regional and limited, theology which is required of us at present. My discussion and criticizing of arguments and theses developed by Latin American theologians are thus intended as an exercise in that mutual accountability between Christians which our common faith and calling both offers and requires. What am I obliged and enabled to say out of my limited location within the tradition and expressions of Christianity and under the pressures of *my* social reality in response to what is being said elsewhere ? This response takes the form both of an acceptance of what is heard and of a criticism of what is heard. I believe that the possibility and necessity of this interchange (through whatever difficulties of conflict, contradiction and incomprehension) is itself an effect, or even an example, of that 'Transcendence in the midst' which is my underlying and central theme. However conditioned may be my receiving of, and response to, the gift and giving of the God who embodied himself in history as Jesus Christ, I do not believe that this God is thereby so conditioned. Rather it is his freedom and transcendence which constitutes the possibility of my limitedness being able to speak to and hear from the human limitedness of others.

I am not, therefore, seeking to call in question particular decisions and commitments. I am rather raising questions about the interpretations and consequences with which these particular decisions or commitments are surrounded. Under the pressure of highly oppressive situations certain Christians have thought it right to go very close to equating the Marxist diagnosis of oppression and the Marxist proposition of class war with the Christian understanding of sin and the Christian call to be part of the struggle of the kingdom against evil and for the salvation of men. Can we accept this close identification for ourselves however much we must try to respect the agony of the realities of human oppression which push our fellow Christians to this identification and however much we must try to face up to the judgment upon our own share in oppression and exploitation? I think we must answer 'no', and explicate this answer in order that we may develop our response to the challenge of political involvement.

Any withdrawal from the issues posed by Marxism about oppression, conflict, and ideology in the name of a Transcendent God, gospel and salvation would seem to be a denial of the way, through Jesus Christ, that Transcendence is expressed in the midst of our oppressions, conflicts and limitations. A love which denies all attention to politics would seem to lose credibility, as refusing to pay attention now to that which causes so many to suffer now. However, a politics which claims an equivalence to love cannot, I think, validly claim the name of Jesus Christ, nor can it truly advance the hope and the glory of men and women.

Is then, the class struggle the same thing as the struggle for the kingdom of God and are the poor and the oppressed the chief, if not the sole, agents of God's saving work in history? There seems to be no biblical promise or hint that the poor liberate themselves or are the liberators. The poor are indeed those who reveal the judgment of God and those of particular concern to the mercy of God. But the source both of judgment and of salvation is God.

It is, I think, particularly significant to consider in their context the passages of which Gutierrez makes use in his chapter on the poor. These include Job 24. Here we have a very powerful description of the plight of the poor which is full of indignation. But this is part of a speech of Job in which he is wrestling to maintain his conviction that God is somehow just and justifiable *despite* the injustices and indifferences of human happenings and behaviour. It offers no hint as to how these are to be overcome. The rest of his Old Testament references, such as Amos 2 and Isaiah 10, are all threats of the judgment which will come *in the day of the Lord* because of the attitude of the rulers and oppressors, manifested in their treatment of the poor. Likewise the passages from the gospel of Luke which are cited as being specially concerned with the condemnation of the rich contain phrases like 'your reward is great *in heaven*' (of the poor – see Luke 6), a condemnation of the man who 'lays up treasure for himself and is not rich toward God' (12.21) and the need to sell all and *follow Jesus* (18.22). In the supporting passages cited from the epistle of James we get the advice to the poor to be patient and wait for the 'parousia', i.e., once again, for the 'day of the Lord' (James 5.7).

The overall tenor of all these passages seems to be quite clearly and simply that justice *will be done* because *God* is just and repentance is called for in the light of this. There seems, thus, to be very good biblical evidence for seeing the signs of injustice, oppression and man's inhumanity to man in these very aspects of social and human life to which the theory of the class struggle also draws sharp and concrete attention. But this is not at all the same thing as providing biblical evidence that the injustice, the oppression and the inhumanity will be *overcome* in the manner indicated and expected by the theory of the class struggle. A close agreement concerning symptoms does not necessarily imply or provide an agreement about cure or salvation. And clearly the crucial question lies here. What shall we do to be saved? And with what hope shall we respond in what way to the situations under judgment and to the realization of the distortions of being human which we suffer and produce. The real struggle is clearly about what sort of saving energies and possibilities there are to which men and women can respond and of which they can be part.

There are no valid grounds for taking the Marxist and Christian understandings of human possibilities and hopes as nearly equivalent or even closely convergent unless it has been decided that neither biblical revelation nor human possibility can have any other reference than the solely historical. But to confine men to history is to condemn man to extinction and to restrict love to history is to commit love to frustration. The Bible is the record of the discovery of a Transcendent God and Jesus, if he is a revolutionary, is a Transcendent one. Of course, all this is known and hoped 'in the midst', i.e., in some sense or other in history. Gutierrez cites J. L. Segundo as writing 'We can say then that Christianity, although like the religions of extraterrestrial salvation because of its absolute salvation, differs from them because it introduced this absolute value into the midst of the historical and apparently profane reality of the existence of man'.[2] This is surely correct and powerfully true of the religion of the incarnation. The absolute of love is introduced right into the midst of history. But that is

[2] *A Theology of Liberation*, p. 179 n. 10.

not to say that either the absolute or the absolute salvation of human existence and human becoming is confined to history.

Christianity as practised and expressed in most of the structures known to us has so often ignored or misunderstood the structures and pressures of history as to render its references to the Transcendent not only incredible but also suspect as a means and source of ideological distortion. This is part of that contradiction of Christianity which is my starting-point, my personal conviction and my continuing theme and perplexity. But it does not seem possible to replace a contradicted vision by an implausible one. Moreover, as I shall go on to argue, the Marxist vision is both limited and dangerous to the fullness of humanity while the Christian vision, if only it were not contradicted by so much practice, takes that fullness both more profoundly and more gloriously. But the contradiction is real and much light is thrown on the realities of this contradiction by the intuitions and some of the aspects of the analyses of Marxism. This is why it has seemed essential to devote the first half of this exploration to examining the justness of much of the Marxist analysis of history and to insist on the concreteness of judgment to be perceived in the actual situation of the poor. Reference to Transcendence in the name and the spirit of Jesus Christ can be no turning away from history. But the following of Jesus Christ remains a possibility of absolutely critical importance because it is not an abandonment to history. And in history no absolute salvation lies.

We must return, therefore, to the points I raised at the conclusion of the last chapter. We have had to delay in expanding them because it is not safe to proceed until one has hammered home the absolute necessity of facing, and continuing to face, judgment from the poor and the excluded in history. Eventual divergence must not be allowed to turn us aside from current convergence. We must accept the force of the judgment in history before we can be set free to respond and witness to the salvation beyond history. Until then the contradiction of Christianity remains crippling. Now, however, it may be possible to proceed positively with the concern with more than history which I believe to be necessary and which is reflected in my statement towards the end of the last chapter (p. 40) that, in the Marxist diagnosis, 'there is a deep error about the nature of human reality and about the relationships and possibilities which are involved in and open to human beings'.

One chief aspect of the error is to confine man to history. The other is to be blind to the complexities of sin. The effect of this compound mistake is an inevitable tendency to a limiting totalitarianism which cannot but add to the dehumanizing forces at work in history and in human relationships. For *history* cannot offer either an assured salvation from all which contradicts and distorts being human nor a salvation which brings truly human fulfilment to men and women as they are to be understood in the light of love, both human and divine.

We are, as I have just said a paragraph or two earlier, faced here with a crucial question 'about what sort of saving energies and possibilities there are to which men and women can respond and of which they can be part'. The form in which this crucial question faces us is as a question about history. The biblical tradition, and any Christian tradition which tries to be faithful to and consistent with this tradition, insists that history has to be taken absolutely seriously as the place and process where men and women discover their possibilities and enter into the making and marring of them. I have further been developing the strong conviction that the Marxist analysis of our human and social performances in history reveals to us critical facets of ways in which our social reality mars the becoming human of the majority of men and women in the world. This Marxist critique provides us with a challenge to and a judgment upon the way in which we express our humanness through our structures, institutions and patterns of behaviour which is strongly convergent with the prophetic strictures of the Bible upon those who oppress and ignore the poor. Indeed these Marxist illuminations provide us with vital and vivid means for understanding and applying the contemporary meaning and requirements of the biblical truths. Thus far, then, we are kept deeply immersed in history and disturbingly reminded that we are required to be part of the struggle in history for overcoming all those obstacles to being and becoming human which are discovered to be contrary to the purposes of love.

So there can be no withdrawal from the lessons learned in history or from the processes of history as the place where human and Christian discipleship must be both learned and worked out. But we have also begun to notice ways in which Marxist intuitions are placed within overall theories or trends which threaten to deny or ignore important aspects of human living. We have also noted that biblical and Marxist insights diverge as well as converge. My suggestion so far is that these difficulties and divergencies will be found to focus round the understanding of history and round the evaluation of sin. My hunch is that here we have reached a sort of watershed in the argument and the exploration. Christians, I think, are bound to deny that in the final analysis, men and women are historical creatures. We, as Christians, must insist that human beings are not shaped by history only and our final fulfilment is not found within history. Our Christian need and right to make this claim about human being and human beings are not overthrown by the contradictions which Christianity has produced and does perpetrate in history. For history is full not only of Christian contradictions but also of many other human contradictions. The problem of these contradictions is also the problem of history and of whether history offers any fulfilment to human beings. The problem of history is also the problem of sin. But the problem of sin cannot be reduced to the problem of history. To reduce everything to history is to dehumanize man and to defraud him of that fulfilment which is also salvation from sin. Marxists have understood very much about injustice but they are in very grave danger of misunderstanding man. Christians have contradicted the vision of men which they have been commissioned to explore and share, not least by failing to understand about injustice. Thus injustice and contradiction remain to be faced in history. But the question remains about how we are to understand history.

That any notion of salvation or liberation solely within history is an impossibility and a delusion is suggested by a variety of considerations which include the following. The historical pressures of the world and its problems are as likely to produce apocalypse as paradise. There is in any case death, standing as the final example of the strict limits with which human beings are faced in history. Once love has glimpsed what is involved in the being of each human being who is loved and capable of loving, it is exceedingly difficult to give any fully human meaning to talk of 'salvation' or 'liberation' which lies in an historical future which is extremely doubtful and which, even if it were reached, would be of no meaning and significance to the dead. It is not Man who loves and is loved but men and women and it is their contradictions which call for salvation, not those of history. Further, to define all human relations solely by reference to alienation, exploitation and oppression, and then to absolutize history and historical structures, is to deny at least equal reality to those inter-personal relationships which are humanly enjoyed and glimpsed despite structures, alienation and historical circumstances. Men and women do experience their humanity in an infinite variety of 'nows'. To locate the meaning, value and fulfilment of these in a hypothetical historical future is to 'flatten' reality in a strangely de-humanizing way, for it is to subordinate love to structures, which is to subordinate the human to the less than human.

This flattening of reality is also reflected in the ways in which, in 'socialist' cultures committed to a theory which absolutizes history, the values revealed in art and contemplation are also relativized away along with values hinted at by inter-personal love and which have already been referred to. These present realities are subordinated to a purely projected future and only 'social realism' is held to be of value. Out of this new forms of oppression come. This leads on to the point that 'history' shows no signs of dealing with wickedness. New forms and corruptions of totalitarianism and power arise. There is, indeed, little reason to expect 'history' to avoid this. If social reality is a human creation, then to ascribe human wickedness solely to the structures of oppression created by human beings is simply to side-step the human problems or to leave us perpetually trapped in them.

Finally, there is the problem of how history on its own will help us to face up to the impossibility personally and the impracticability historically of the demands both of the gospel and of the revolution. Where will truly victorious neighbourly love come from in a world such as ours ? And where will 'the new man' come from, since it is the present man who has to love and to change, to promote the revolution and be revolutionized ?

5

The hopefulness of solidarity in sin

As I wrote towards the end of the last chapter, I suspect that we are now at a watershed in the exploration and the argument. The watershed is represented by our having to face the questions of how we understand history and whether we understand and respond to being and becoming human as completely confined to history. This cruciality of the question of history obliged me to expend some space at the end of the last chapter in gathering together the threads from the exploration so far which converge on this issue. So that we may go on with the exploration as effectively and as realistically as possible I propose, before I proceed further, to locate this summary with regard to history within a summary explanation of how I see the whole exploration as having developed so far.

I am conducting an exercise and exploration in white bourgeois English theology – in the hope that our own needs will enable us to develop a theology that is our own, that is to say, in the hope that we may achieve an understanding of God and his purposes which makes available to us the saving, freeing transcendence of God in the midst of the conditioned and disturbing realities of our historical situation, and, in particular, in the midst of the contradictions which we both promote and suffer.

The situation is that we are trapped in tribalisms which deny both a common humanity and a universal gospel. This is the first dilemma – our Western Christianity is contradicted – but shall we deny Christ? This is a humanly critical question because there is a Christian vision of a universal and glorious humanity and it would be a denial of a unique hope for humanity to turn aside from this. Are the implications of love to be denied? This is the second dilemma. In the face of these dilemmas I have turned to consider especially the Marxist critique of society. This is a lively and widely influential diagnosis of our condition which seems to provide a realistic probe into the ways in which our society conditions us and into ways in which man is set against man. It may be that in receiving judgment we may be enabled to find ways for repentance and redirection which resolve our dilemmas and give us hope. If we can discover the sources of wrongness among us then we may have found ways of putting things right.

Moreover the judgment pointed to by the Marxist critique is certainly reinforced by the biblical treatment of the poor and the excluded from society. Thus, important aspects of Marxist intuitions about the contradictions in our society are convergent with the prophetic message of the Bible. Nevertheless, in its absolutizing both of history and of its own interpretation of history Marxism would seem to threaten humanity and to ignore the full dimensions of reality.

I have been slow fully to come to grips with this last point because I am convinced that we cannot, hopefully as human beings or faithfully as Christians, go beyond the Marxist analysis and message – as I am sure we must – unless and until we face the truth of judgment contained in them. As I have tried to indicate in my brief discussion of God as the Disturber in the previous chapter this, for me, is itself a theological judgment. I believe that the pattern of God's dealing with men as revealed in the Bible shows that the way to receiving the realities of his salvation lies through the facing and accepting of his judgment. We shall be able to overcome our contradictions if, and only if, we face them and see how they point us to ways in which we are denying our own humanity by denying, distorting and ignoring the humanity of others. I further believe that it is God who gives the presence, the relationships and the strength for that acceptance of judgment which is required for us to be changed into more human and hopeful ways of living and responding. This last point – concerning our dependence on God for the ability to receive the condemnation and renewal which is needed if we are to be part of human fulfilment and divine salvation – is really the critical thesis of the second half of this exploration. But I anticipate the argument a little in order to underline and explain the amount of time spent in investigating the force of the Marxist diagnosis and judgment.

If we go on to draw attention to more than is contained in that diagnosis and judgment and, in the light of that more, to criticize the very foundations of the Marxist approach, at all costs we must not think that such a procedure entitles us to set on one side the sharp, historical specific and radical judgment on our society and on our own ideas and behaviour which Marxism expresses. To evade any of this, and here I return to my insistence that what I am expressing is a theological conviction, will be to refuse to face up to the judgment of God and therefore to betray his salvation and to deprive ourselves of a part in the liberation, newness and opportunities which he is offering us. Transcendence in the midst does not operate in such a way as to blur or obliterate the human, historical and political realities in the midst of which we encounter or discover this Transcendence. Rather these realities are made clearer with both their challenges and their possibilities sharpened. We are thereby required to grow out of our fantasies, our excuses and our falsities, whether they have received their plausible or taken-for-granted shape from Christianity, from Marxism or from any other source. The importance of Marxism for our exercise and exploration in white bourgeois English theology is that it provides intuitions and insights which reveal fantasies and falsities which are particularly those of our church and our Christianity. We respond to these analyses therefore as part of theological discernment and Christian obedience. This does not, however, require an uncritical acceptance of the whole construction of the Marxist argument and dialectic. Marxism is not capable of replacing Christianity nor can it be successfully argued that Marxism in some sense provides the necessary and appropriate modern interpretation and application of Christianity. Marxism is a most important source, perhaps the most important modern source at this point in history, for correcting Christianity and recalling Christians to their biblical insights and vocation. But for a Christian the reasons for taking Marxism with the utmost seriousness and accepting many of its insights are theological and not Marxist. This is so because the Christian understanding of reality is and must remain theological (that is to say based on an understanding of and response to God) and not Marxist (that is to say based on theories of the atheist Marx). None the less I am convinced that it is theologically essential to accept the insights of Marxism to which I have been drawing attention and that this requires certain practical responses which I shall discuss later. It is with this understanding that I now attempt to go on and explain more fully why the Christian, whatever his individual or corporately shared sinfulness, must challenge the Marxist as being neither realistically hopeful nor sufficiently human.

The Marxist is not realistically hopeful because he appears to assume that a state of affairs fulfilling human beings can, and indeed will, emerge out of present conflicts within the historical series and solely under the dynamism of that series. He is not sufficiently human because he restricts the scope of human relationships and possibilities to a limited and limiting range of historical situations understood solely in terms of the ideology of exploitation and liberation. I have already drawn attention to the fact that what is at issue is a basic understanding of reality, of what energies are at work in the universe. At this level of understanding I do not myself believe that the Christian vision and understanding can be demonstrated to be true. Rather we have an offer of faith and a claim to commitment the evidence for the truth and authenticity of which lies in the response experienced and the fulfilment which will be entered into. We have found ourselves having to refer more and more often to a basic understanding of reality and to the question of what energies are at work in the universe. It will, I believe, become even more obvious as we proceed that practical diagnoses about the responses required or available to human problems cannot be separated from visions, theories or beliefs about the true context within which human living is set and so about the extent and nature of the network of energies to which human beings are open. The implications and scope of a Christian version have already been given in a preliminary discussion in chapter 2. One of the ways in which Christianity and Marxism show a certain convergence is that they both, in their respective ways, continue to insist that there are ways of understanding and responding to reality which offer men and women prospects and promises of fulfilment. Clearly a critical and ever-present question is why Christians or Marxists should feel able and obliged to persevere in their assertions and in their continuing search for the implications and applications of them. To this I propose to turn in the next chapter.

At present and in the course of my exploration I am claiming that it is humanly urgent and necessary to call in question certain Marxist implications and I am doing so on a basis which is mixed. I find myself calling attention to features of the human situation which Marxism seems to ignore or distort. Now, am I claiming that anyone can see such features and should be able to see that they do not fit in with Marxist analysis? Or am I really assuming Christian insights and thus finding that it is the perspective provided by these insights which helps me to pick out these features which will not fit in and which gives the hints for understanding their wider significance? My own view of my own view is, as I have already said, that it is a mixed one. For example, I believe that anyone ought to be able to see that human achievements in love and in art severely question the adequacy of Marxist theories about history and about structures. However, the significance I give to this questioning and the line of exploration and explanation which this prompts me to develop are clearly the result of my Christian perspectives. Further, the more I attempt to give positive descriptions or make positive proposals rather than to be merely critical of the descriptions and proposals of others, the more I am obliged to take my Christian insights as principal guides for my exploration. Hence the importance of the question about where these Christian insights come from. Where do we gain the idea, the hope and the faith that 'God is known in his giving' (see chapter 2) or that talk about 'Transcendence in the midst' is a worthwhile form of stuttering about real possibilities ? Again, it may be possible to see that Marxism on its own does not deal with the contradictions of men and women and provokes various contradictions of its own. But so does Christianity. For this was where we started. So what does one draw on to encourage and authorize a continuing exploration which claims both to be guided by certain insights into reality and at the same time to be a search for the meaning and the validation of these insights ?

It would therefore seem necessary to pause at some stage in the particular exploration on which we are at present engaged in order to give some sort of account of the source of the insights which are being both brought to bear on, and put to the test of, the problems we are encountering. For the basic presuppositions of this exploration of mine are clearly not the contradictions which actually provoked me to start out but the Christian vision, insights and hopes which I find to be contradicted. Yet, contradicted as I find them, I find also that I am constantly appealing to them and bringing them into play. As I have pointed out above, vision, faith and hope are not capable of having their truthfulness and reality decisively demonstrated. They can only be demonstrated and pursued to authentication or to destruction. But since the claim is that the content of the vision, the reality of faith and the direction of life are of essential significance with regard to our understanding of the possibilities of human beings in and in relation to history, it is clearly necessary to give some account of how they arise in history and what shape they give to the understanding of history. I propose therefore to devote the following chapter to developing such an account as the need for this seems to have arisen out of the exploration as it has developed. Meanwhile I shall complete this chapter by leaving on one side this question of the mixed sources of the understandings and insights which I am using and simply return to my critique of the Marxist understanding of the human on which I have found myself launched. This is in order to take the exploration to a stage at which it can rest ready to be taken up again when we have had a look at the sources and shaping of the Christian insights which I am finding myself obliged to weave constantly into the argument. While, then, I do not hold that the truth of Christian hopes for man can be demonstrated, but only pointed to and pursued, I do believe that the Marxist expectations concerning man can be shown to be false and that in at least three respects.

First, Marxist theory limits the significance of human experience to a too narrowly historical frame, with history interpreted in a constricting way. Secondly, and in contrast to the first point, Marxism ignores certain limits on human actions and possibilities which make it impossible to expect fulfilment within history alone of the potentialities and promises inherent in men and women. Thirdly, there are areas of human experience and achievement which Marxist theory in practice either ignores or minimizes in the interests of a projected and hypothetical future. In all this I believe that Marxists are wrong about the nature of the reality and energy which composes man and his context. Discernment of the structural and ideological obstacles which loom so large in our being and becoming human has been erected into a total principle for interpreting human and historical reality which deprives man of his true glory.

Before I proceed to develop this may I yet again strengthen my repeated interpolations to the effect that I do not wish to turn aside, or to turn aside from, the judgments which I believe Marxism to be instrumental in bringing to bear on our history and society. Chapter 8 in particular will be devoted to trying to show how one might attempt to hold together a large acceptance of Marxist diagnosis of symptoms with a fundamental rejection of Marxist beliefs about cures – or should we say 'salvation'. At this point I would like also to add that this fundamental disagreement about ultimates which we are now having more and more to face does not exclude very close co-operation in particular situations and for particular political ends.

Indeed, I should like to suggest that one important manifestation of Transcendence in the midst is to be found in the way in which commitment to human situations can be found to take us far beyond what we hold to be our fundamental ideas – so that we discover possibilities and develop hopes that we never dreamt of. It would be a betrayal of Christian faith to be afraid of collaboration with Marxists where the particular oppression of a political situation and the particular aims of a short- or medium-term strategy required it. For the concern of any faith related to Jesus Christ is, surely, not the truth of Christianity or Marxism but rather the opening up of human beings to more hope of, and more enjoyment in, that being and becoming human which is understood as the gift and the promise of God. In the pursuit of this aim there can arise both the possibility of collaboration in particular situations and for particular aims and the need of confrontation about wider contexts and continuing purposes. If Christians and Marxists can challenge one another to transcend their own limitations in and for the sake of the struggle to be human, then we shall have at least some contribution to the discovery of whether men and women are responding to more than the image of their own hopes imposed on and sought after in history, for some aspect of this 'more' will be discovered through the very challenges.

My thesis, then, is that history is not enough for being human and herein I believe that I stand in the Christian tradition and point to the Christian gospel. As a way into developing this thesis I suggest we consider the parable of the sheep and the goats at the end of Matthew 25, since this is often used nowadays as showing that our relation to Jesus and his kingdom is to be found, and to be found solely, by our commitment to that historical action for the poor and the oppressed which is, allegedly, the mainspring of Marxist action. Since my exploration is attempting to proceed by an attempt to see, and to see into, certain features of our human being, it is necessary to set out the parable here for reflection in the hope that it will evoke our sensitivity for the sort of reflective questioning of ourselves and of our human environment which is required.

But when the Son of man shall come in his glory, and all the angels with him, then shall he sit on the throne of his glory: and before him shall be gathered all the nations: and he shall separate them one from another, as the shepherd separateth the sheep from the goats: and he shall set the sheep on his right hand, but the goats on the left. Then shall the King say unto them on his right hand, Come, ye blessed of my Father, inherit the kingdom prepared for you from the foundation of the world: for I was an hungred, and ye gave me meat: I was thirsty, and ye gave me drink: I was a stranger, and ye took me in; naked, and ye clothed me: I was sick, and ye visited me: I was in prison, and ye came unto me. Then shall the righteous answer him, saying, Lord, when we saw thee an hungred, and fed thee? or athirst, and gave thee drink? And when saw we thee a stranger, and took thee in? or naked, and clothed thee? And when saw we thee sick, or in prison, and came unto thee? And the King shall answer and say unto them, Verily I say unto you, Inasmuch as ye did it unto one of these my brethren, even these least, ye did it unto me. Then shall he say also unto them on the left, Depart from me, ye cursed, into the eternal fire which is prepared for the devil and his angels; for I was an hungred, and ye gave me no meat: I was thirsty, and ye gave me no drink: I was a stranger, and ye took me not in; naked and ye clothed me not; sick, and in prison, and ye visited me not. Then shall they also answer, saying, Lord, when saw we thee an hungred, or athirst, or a stranger, or naked, or sick, or in prison, and did not minister unto thee? Then shall he answer them, saying, Verily I say unto you, Inasmuch as ye did it not unto one of these least, ye did it not unto me. And these shall go away into eternal punishment; but the righteous into eternal life (Matt. 25.31–46).

What are we to hear in this parable? Simply a devastating description of who is righteous and who is not, of who can hope to share in the kingdom and who can expect nothing but condemnation? Or have we also to hear that which was articulated by Paul when he wrote, for example, 'All have sinned, and fall short of the glory of God' (Rom. 3.23)? I ask this question for two, not unconnected, reasons.

First, if the parable is solely and simply describing those who will enjoy the kingdom, then it is clear that the kingdom is confined to a very few heroes and I am certainly not among them. As far as I myself am concerned it may be retorted that I have here grounds for concern, but not for questioning the general validity of the interpretation. But the point does not concern me only and leads in to the second difficulty. If there are those who take this parable as a command to action, which command they believe they can fulfil, then it seems to me that such people are either alarmingly self-righteous about their own motives, possibilities and effects or else dangerously insensitive to what is fully involved in loving their neighbour. Can we realistically maintain that either the gospel or the revolution are feasible human attainments in the light of what we now experience of human behaviour? All this is connected with the points I have already listed as indicating 'the sort of things which make the notion of salvation or liberation solely within history an impossibility'. In particular, I am taking up the last point, viz.: 'How does or will history on its own help us to face the impossibility personally and the impracticability historically of the demands both of the gospel and of the revolution. . . . Where will "the new man" come from, since it is the present man who has to love, and to change, to promote the revolution and to be revolutionized?' (p. 58).

If we sincerely examine ourselves in the mirror of our relationships with other people and if we seriously reflect on what we know about other people in their relationships to one another, how can we suppose that we or they are those who will build unaided, and simply by our mutual efforts, the Kingdom of Man? Our problem is man's inhumanity to man, compounded by man's exploitation of the physical possibilities of his world. Let us leave aside this second feature, important as it is, as being another side of self-centred human exploitiveness and concentrate on man's direct inhumanity to man. Will this be dealt with by a rigorous application of the imperative assumed to be the sole point of the parable of the sheep and the goats?

The poor are exploited, the poor are ignored and more poor are produced. But man's inhumanity to man is not confined to what might be called vertical relationships between exploiters and exploited. It is certainly also to be found, as we might say, horizontally between so-called exploiters themselves and between the poor themselves. Of course, it can be contended that this distortion of horizontal relationships is brought about by the vertical distortions of the relationship between the exploited and the exploiters. The exploiters in their inhumanity distort their own humanity and so, of course, are inhuman to one another, while the poor are made inhuman by their exploitation and so, of course, are inhuman to one another. I believe there is much truth in this. But surely it is not anything like the whole truth. As a total explanation it is dangerously dehumanizing, for it gravely underestimates both human wickedness and human love and creativity in history. As I have already suggested human being and becoming are both more limited and less limited than this theory recognizes.

Let us develop the argument from the positive end, that is, from the ubiquity of man's capacity to love. This is certainly the correct move theologically, for however much the doctrine of sin has been sinfully distorted and abused it is in fact a doctrine which asserts the highest possible value for man by relating him directly to the glory of God. The theological way to approach man's negative qualities is, therefore, through his positive ones. What all doctrines and explanations of human being and becoming which rely totally on historical and structural analysis neglect is what men and women sometimes achieve or experience in their personal relationships whatever the historical or structural conditions. Every argument about structural alienation, societal violence and historical process which will liberate men and women must have its echoes, dimensions and effects checked against and affected by an awareness of what a face-to-face human relationship is, can be and can achieve now, and under a vast range of circumstances which cannot be theoretically defined in advance.

Perhaps I can indicate the insight or intuition which I am hoping will be perceived by being explicitly autobiographical. I was once discussing forms of local community action with someone whom I had only just met for the first time. Despite this we seemed to get rapidly and easily into a discussion in which we shared our motivations and hopes as well as our doubts and near despair. The sensitivity of this person both to human problems and experiences and to human achievements in the arts and literature seemed to me to be of a very high order. This made the discussion, for me, both illuminating and disturbing. At some point the question came up about the conflicts people encounter between what they experience in inter-personal relationships and what is either forced upon them by political and social structures or required of them in fighting against these structures. In the course of explaining this perennial and, as I think, never soluble tension and conflict my newly-met friend said that, in the last analysis, one had always to come down on the side of the political and social pressures and action, for it was the political and social which was finally determinative of reality. Now I cannot believe this and I further hold that, for the sake of humanity, one must not believe this. But without a realistic conception of sin it seems to me that one will always be in danger of being forced to abandon the personal for the structural and jettison love until 'the future'.

I do not intend, in the argument I am pursuing here, either to deny the necessity for political action guided by a realistic assessment of structural realities or to suggest that political action can avoid doing harm to some human beings both in their selves and in their relation-ships. Any decision to fight against intolerable oppression illustrates this dilemma in a sharp form. Power, it seems, cannot be redistributed painlessly and campaigns for particular objects can scarcely avoid side effects which are neither wanted nor desirable. I see, therefore, no chance of political action being invariably and consistently human, no matter how much it is directed to what are held to be ultimately humanizing ends. Nor, as I have said before repeatedly, do I see any gospel of love withdrawing from any concern with political action and remaining credible or, indeed, consistent with itself.

What I do see as essential is the need to face the contradictory and ambivalent nature of political actions and to refuse any attempt to dissolve this internal contradiction away by claiming that political realities have priority over human interrelational realities in determining the ultimate nature of things and for discerning the ultimate values and meanings inherent in human living. Here we are back to the clash about the ultimate nature of the reality of which we are part. And here too, I believe, we have the first clue to the importance of that to which I am trying to point by the title of this chapter, 'The hopefulness of solidarity in sin'. It is absolutely essential to retain the conviction and awareness that acts which are dehumanizing, inhuman and less than fully human, remain precisely that even when they are politically essential or in-evitable or, at least, held to be so. The attitude of the oppressed in hating his oppressor and the act of the oppressed in imprisoning, terrorizing or killing his oppressor do not become human and human-izing because they are part of a historical process of liberation, which liberation may, as a whole, be held to be just, justified and hopeful. (On this, see further chapter 9.)

At the interrelational level all such transactions between human beings are sinful. That is to say, they fall short of the glory and the possibility which are open to human beings and due to human beings as such, that is, as persons with human faces, which faces can reflect love, however much the actuality both of their social conditions and of their internal attitudes may have made the faces both distorted and distorting. Nothing must be made into a justification for seeing anything less in a human face than a human being, not even the evident fact that this or those human beings have never recognized the human faces of those whom they oppress. A historical situation which requires or enables the oppressed to fight the oppressor and the poor to overcome the rich does not thereby produce a temporary race of privileged humans whose acts of violence, hate and power became human and humanizing because they are fighting for the underprivileged against privileged exploiters. For men are not constituted by history alone or for history alone. They are constituted by and for love.

This means that men and women are that which their relationships enable them to become and the primary and constitutive relationships are the face-to-face ones and not the structural and historical ones. Hence the relationships of violence and destruction which the political fight for historical freedom may render inevitable cannot become or be thought of as even indifferent, let alone good. They are sinful. There is hope to be found in them and through them only if we may perceive, and keep our sense of, our solidarity in sin. To welcome, license and justify less than fully human actions performed for the sale of liberating a wider humanness is to invite and probably to guarantee a self-righteous tyranny which is convinced that the agents of the good fight are thereby guaranteed as good in ideology, intention and achievement so that all deviation or fundamentally dissenting judgment is, by definition, bad and anti-human and so justifiably dealt with by inhuman means. Unless sinfulness is recognized as something shared in by all human beings, then there is no escape from the dehumanizing limitations of false and premature absolutes proclaimed by limited and partial agents of a partially understood historical process.

But can I state more clearly what I mean by 'sinfulness'? I have already indicated that by sinful actions I mean those which fall short of the glory and possibility which are open to human beings and due to human beings. I am, clearly, attempting to 'draw into the midst' of human affairs and human understanding that definition of sin which I have already quoted from St Paul: 'For all have sinned and fall short of the glory of God.' To explicate fully what I am trying to point to I shall need the rest of my lectures, not least the discussion of man as in the image of God.

Nevertheless I believe that one of the great sources of at least potential awareness of Transcendence in the midst is what can be seen in human faces as reflecting human being, when face speaks and responds to face, by no means necessarily with words, but by contact of eye and exchange of expression and gesture. Here is already more than a glimmer and a hint of the glory and possibility which are open to human beings and due to human beings. It is precisely because of this glory, and possibility, which is in human beings and their capacity for relationships, and not in 'history', that the passionate need arises to fight in history for some liberation and freeing in history from all that distorts and denies these relationships, these possibilities and this glory. But this fight can involve just as much contradiction of what is being fought for as the very contradictions which have to be fought against. Unless this is recognized and reckoned with, it will be the contradictions which are victorious and not that humanizing which is being fought for.

But this present tendency and contradiction reduces both history and the being and becoming human which is experienced in history to nonsense only if history is absolutized and held to contain the total clues both to the resources available in history and the fulfilment to be achieved through history. If all we have and shall ever have is 'history', then two courses only lie open. On the one hand the contradictions experienced in history must be rationalized to a point where their source can be found in something so over-simplified as 'exploitation'. This allows apparent hope to be kept alive in history but at the cost of a dehumanizing and unrealistic limitation of both the threats and the possibilities that are involved in being human. Alternatively, it may be concluded that the contradictions dominate and that there is no ultimate meaning, either in their history or beyond, to the possibilities glimpsed in human living and human loving.

But neither of these dehumanizing alternatives is forced upon us, because it is not true that all we have is history. This, basically, is what the much misunderstood and much misused symbol of the Fall stands for. As J. V. Taylor puts it: 'The myth of man's first disobedience and its cosmic outcome is, above everything else, a ringing assertion that the nature of ultimate reality cannot be deduced from the totality of existence as we know it.'[1] On the basis of the revelation and the gospel given to

[1] *The Go-between God*, SCM Press and Fortress Press 1972, p. 74.

them, but given for all men, Christians confront both those Oriental religions and philosophies which deny that nature and history contribute to ultimate significance and those Western ideologies and philosophies such as Marxism and scientific humanism, which confine ultimate significance to nature and to history. But the key to this confrontation lies in the understanding of man as the sinner who is falling short of the divine glory which is destined to be the measure and the enjoyment of human glory.

Before I turn aside to discuss where this understanding of man comes from, I wish to give four indications of ways in which an understanding of 'solidarity in sin' as a crucial dimension to human being and becoming sets us free to be both more realistic about man in history and more realistically hopeful for man than does the Marxist straight-jacket.

First, it sets us free to assert the primacy of personal relationships over historical structures, whether economic, social or political, and thus to do justice to the claim that it is love and not the dynamics of either history or nature which is the fundamental energy of the universe. To understand man as sinner is to make his personal dynamics and personal relationships the basic and defining features of him without in any way denying the distortions, difficulties, partialities and problems of these dynamics and relationships. 'Wrongness' at these inter-human relationships is not to be side-tracked to non-human causes such as structural ones, whatever part such structural distortions and oppressions can legitimately be shown to have played and be playing. It is vital not to 'side-track' 'wrongness' away in such a fashion because this also mis-locates what is 'right' about man, namely, his capacity for personal relationships. (This is a point of central importance to which we shall return in chapter 7.) To retain any grounds for claiming absolute value for man as personal one must, in some sense, recognize man as sinner, i.e., with the roots of his 'wrongness' in himself – but without that fact thereby defining him as essentially wrong or absurd.

This first indication slides into the second, which is that the under-standing of solidarity in sin sets us free to give unreserved approbation and value to all human achievements in the field of art, of aesthetics, of the spirit and of love under whatever circumstances and by whoever achieved. Nothing shows up the essentially dehumanizing meanness of Marxist totalitarianism more sharply than the attitudes to cultural achievement shown in both Soviet and Chinese Marxist thinking. Ideological correctness (according to the current fashion) must be displayed if art or literature is to be approved and enjoyed. But this is plainly nasty nonsense. You do not have to be ideologically or proletarianly pure either to love well or to design, write, create or make music well. The human spirit and human aesthetics triumph again and again in sin. But this does not, of itself, negate the sin.

From one proper human perspective it is intolerable that great works of art and other great human achievements should be worked at and enjoyed by privileged and exploitive minorities. But to deny them to be the great and glorious things they are is to deny humanity. What has to be held together is both the glory and the sinful sense of privilege and exploitation. (This can be done, only, I believe by some understanding of reality which includes a vision and reality of cross and passion. But this aspect of the matter must be left until later.)

A third indication of the freedom offered us by recognition of sin is the ability to face up to the existence of wickedness and of the absolute danger of any absolute power or absolute sense of rightness. On the one hand our hopefulness about the fulfilment of man is not overthrown by the fact, for example, that every good scientific discovery and technological application or every progressive political revolution suffers diversion and distortion. Nor on the other hand are we obliged unrealistically to deny the capacity for wrong doing and wrong thinking among all exponents of all theories and exercises of power. We can further face the truly awful potentiality for tyranny, torture and inflexibility which any position of power can give rise to. Because we know all men are sinners we do not have to pretend. We are also free to fight for limitations to the power of governments and officials without thereby claiming that democracy and its measures are anywhere truly democratic or justly social.

Finally, a recognition of solidarity in sin is a realistic recognition of a true human solidarity. We do all have a share in both that which traps us and the suffering of thus being trapped. Our present enemy cannot justly be made a scapegoat for all from which we suffer nor can our present attacker be rightly seen as the sole source of threats to us. And in any case we are all human beings. Thus being human is not denied and cancelled out by the fact that people have ways of being human which deny the being human of others.

The class struggle or, perhaps, some form of division between human beings closely analogous to that pointed to by the concept of the class struggle, may well be the sharpest pointer we have to the judgment we must perceive and receive upon our society and societies. The notion of the class struggle and its accompanying ideology, however, neither rightly defines human realities nor correctly diagnoses human hopes. In order to develop further what I believe to be a more human and more

Christian response to and in this struggle to be human, we must investigate what Christians may urge about the resources for and possibilities of being human. My approach will be built around the symbols of 'image of God' and 'kingdom of God'. But first, as I have already indicated, we must turn aside to consider the source and process from which these symbols emerge and which can give us encouragement and authorization for their use in the midst of our historical struggles to be human.

6

'Always be ready with an explanation
for anyone who asks you for
the grounds and shape of the hope
that is in you' – (I Peter 3.15)

At the beginning of chapter 2, having stated the dilemma I found myself in because of the contradiction of my Christianity I posed the question 'Why, then, do I not get rid . . . of my dilemma by divesting myself of my Christian faith and my Christian community?' My answer then was that this would be to repudiate a known Giver, Giving and Gift. In order to explain this I launched into a description of a Christian understanding of being human as the gift of God. In the course of this description I made some reference to the way in which this insight on being human was built up through the history and experience of the people of Israel and then by the people who came to believe in Jesus. I thus gave some indication of how there came into existence that Christian understanding of possibilities and that Christian use of symbols about the realities of God and of man which I have been drawing on all through this exploration and of which I am proposing to make a great deal of use in the rest of the book.

But the indications given in chapter 2 do not seem sufficient to carry us through the exploration in which we are engaged. As the exploration has gone on, I have found myself comparing and contrasting Marxist claims about and insights into human and historical reality with Christian claims. Towards the end of chapter 4 (see p. 56) I found that 'we have reached a sort of watershed in the argument and the exploration', focused particularly on the understanding we should have of men and women as historical beings. This I took up at the beginning of the last chapter and found myself making very firm assertions about the necessity for dependence on God and the historical and human implications of the possibilities offered by God. I also wrote,

'Marxism is not capable of replacing Christianity' (p. 61). I added: 'The Christian understanding of reality is and must remain theological (that is to say based on an understanding of and response to God) and not Marxist (that is to say based on the theories of the atheist Marx).'

This necessity to make statements about 'what energies are at work in the universe' in the form of stark counter-assertions to Marxist theories rather pulled me up short. I am going on to develop Christian insights and Christian symbols in as positive a way as I can to cast light on the struggles, hopes and contradictions through which we all attempt to make something of our being human. In chapter 9 (pp. 133 ff.) when attempting to deal with questions about violence it will be necessary to face the fact (as I believe it to be) that there is no escape from, and no satisfactory explanation of, situations which contradict both our humanity and our Christianity. Yet I shall go on to maintain there are Christian insights and symbols which have power to transcend even such situations. This confrontation between Marxist theories, human contradictions and Christian insights and symbols seems to require something more than mere assertion and exposition for its proper development.

As I have been developing this account of an investigation, a controversy and a process of which we are all a part, I have been hearing growing echoes of some such question as the following. 'We know where Marxist theory and practice comes from. Where does Christian theory and practice come from?' This question does not simply echo in my reflections and cut across them as if it were being posed by opponents, supporters or neutrals from outside. It becomes a question posed within myself. For I am in fact insisting on Christian theory and searching for Christian practice over against Marxist theory and, probably, over against much of Marxist practice. I have alleged theological grounds for endorsing and responding to certain Marxist intuitions, although I have argued that it is the Marxist development of these intuitions which is responsible for these insights being so powerfully available to us. Further, I started from the contradiction of Christianity, although it is now the insights of Christianity which I am claiming to be crucial in a confrontation about the possibilities of history and the nature of the energies at work in the universe. What, then, is the basis for what I am doing? What account do I give of 'the grounds and shape of the hope' (my version of I Peter 3.15) which is guiding my investigation and my argument?

This type of question does not arise at this particular stage of this particular exploration because of an apologetic necessity to establish the truth of what I am saying. I have already written 'Truth here is not something which we can grasp but that of which we may know ourselves to be a part' (p. 12). Men and women have to decide for themselves what truth and reality there is and how they should respond. What can and must be done is to bear witness to truth and reality discovered in the hope of assisting others to like discoveries. Further, in the light of what has been discovered false claims to truth and reality have to be combated. But how can we handle this matter of 'false claim to truth' and 'combating false views of reality' in a humane and responsible way? I believe myself to be entering into both a dialogue and a controversy with Marxists for the sake of humanity, that of myself and all my fellow men and women. I claim a vision of truth and reality which ought to both guide and compel me in this dialogue and controversy and I have been trying to spell out something of this guidance and compulsion. I want to give the rest of the book to developing this further. Yet, as I have already said in several ways, I am clear that I cannot establish the truth of my claim to be responding to truth. I have to bear witness to God, I cannot demonstrate him. But unless I give some account of how this compulsion and hope comes upon me, I feel in very grave danger of apparently contributing one more set of elaborately arranged noises to the babel of fantasies which a small number of the human race incessantly attempt to impose upon the rest of it.

Here I return to something I wrote in the last chapter. I there stated that we were not concerned with 'the truth of Christianity or Marxism but rather (with) the opening up of human beings to more hope of, and more enjoyment in, the possibilities of their being and becoming human' (p. 64). What is of fundamental importance is human beings, men and women, all persons including ourselves, and not theories, visions or doctrines about being human, except in so far as they are related and relatable to the promotion of being human. People have often pursued arguments and constructed theories about what it is to be human as one more manifestation of that dehumanizing distortion which is discussed in chapter 1. Christianity is contradicted because Christians have so often used Christian theories to oppress or to ignore men and women rather than to be part of setting them free. I am concerned to argue against the overall theories of Marxism on the grounds that they constitute a threat to being human. So the whole investigation is about what is available and what is at work to help men and women to be human. An eclectic criticism of one set of theories in the light of another set of theories would scarcely contribute more than one or two slight insights to this main concern and would hardly face up to it with the passionate seriousness it deserves. It cannot be human to do nothing but theorize while men and women die unnecessarily, are distorted and are ignored. So the questions which we must seek to answer are those such as 'What can be done?', 'How can we endure?', 'What may be worked for and hoped for?' These are questions about power, about possibilities, about energies.

Discussion about whether men and women are dehumanized if they are understood as being wholly confined to and by history must therefore be discussion about whether there are powers, possibilities and energies which go beyond history. Talk about 'Transcendence in the midst' is used precisely to refer to such powers and energies. But this brings us back to the insights and practices behind and implied by such talk. How do we get onto such insights and what encourages us in the practice of them?

This is not quite the same question as 'How do we know that they are true?' because claims to have insights into the overall nature of reality and its possibilities are not capable of final demonstration and cannot have simple tests of truth and falsity. It is rather a question about what persuades us to commit ourselves to such insights and practices as relating us to the truth and as providing opportunities for entering into the truth. This is a question about reliability, credibility, trustworthiness, attractiveness. It is necessary to start, and reflect on, some sort of answer to this sort of question, whether or not the answer persuades other people, or even always satisfies oneself. This necessity arises out of the respect and reverence which is prima facie due to men and women in their struggles and their hopes. Men and women should not be bamboozled and exploited. They are. And that by men and women. This is the basic contradiction we are having to face. But the very fact that we find it so basic a contradiction shows that we know that they do not deserve this. So an account must be given of the grounds and shape of the hope that is in us so that we may be accountable and not irresponsible. It seems to me to be a very terrible thing for someone to be determined to fight for his vision at all costs and to become, in his thought and practice, accountable only to this vision and theory and not to his fellow human beings. Along this way both humanity and truth are lost. This, too, is probably the way to the deepest contradictions of the humane intentions of both Christianity and Marxism.

It is considerations like these which push me to this 'giving account' now that I am right in the middle of my main argument and exploration about our contradictions, the understanding we should have of them and the resources with which we can face them. It is not so much that the argument requires it but that the human process of which one is a part requires it. Indeed, I think I can say that I am afraid of my arguing at the same time as I am happy to find myself compelled to argue along the way I am going.

I am afraid of my arguing because it might be false and be so wholly a matter of fantasy and refusal to face realities that it is one more contribution to the confusing and misleading of human beings. And I believe that men and women, just because of who they are, ought not to be misled. Then, again, I am afraid because, whether or not my arguing is pointing towards truth or is supporting falsity, I may be arguing simply out of a desire to maintain or re-establish the 'rightness' of myself and my group. There are so many grounds for being fearful about people who claim to 'know better' than others or to be right over against others. People who know better so often seem to find ways of acting which ensure that others fare worse. Supposed and privileged knowledge seems so often to promote pride rather than to enable humility and the way to selfless self-assertion in the furthering, and in the further pursuit of, the truth glimpsed seems to be very hard to find.

There is also a positive reason for fear which is connected with the reason for being happy that I find myself obliged to follow this way and pursue this argument. This arises from the awe and wonder evoked by the contents and implications of the vision so far seen. The combination of the promise of God glimpsed through Jesus and the possibilities of human beings glimpsed through contemplation of what, even in our contradictions, we are and manage to achieve, suggests a vision of fulfilling and ultimately fulfilled reality which is glorious, holy and worshipful. Therefore when I am exploring an argument about the human and divine possibilities of which we are or may be a part and when I am investigating policies and practices for responding to these possibilities, there is an obligation to proceed with fear and with reverence. Being afraid of my arguing is part of my awareness of, and commitment to, the realities which are the subject of the argument. I am investigating both the contradiction of a Christianity which makes claims about the eternal energies of love and also the contradiction of human beings who are, in themselves, claims for the possibilities of love. It is, therefore, clearly necessary to be afraid that I may simply add to these contradictions. There seems to be no total safeguard against this. All that can be done is to give some description of how and where one is alerted to the energies which one believes to exist and to the vision which one claims must be taken into account.

This description and giving account may give some indication of the basis on which one dares, despite fears and in the midst of contradictions, to contend for the truth and application of insights about men and women derived from faith in God, kindled and directed through Jesus. In particular it may serve to give some indication of what leads me to the central claim and risk of faith, the faith, that is, which is 'through Jesus Christ'. This is the claim that 'through Jesus Christ' we are put in touch with, pointed to and confronted by that which is the defining and determining energy of the whole of the universe. Such a claim can be stated and explored only in language that is pictorial or mythological. But the claim is always being made that the pictures drawn and the stories told are about the way things really are and the way they really will be. Thus the risk has to be taken of looking for ways of relating these pictures and stories decisively and radically to both facts and the future. It is out of the courage and the risk of faith of this quality that there arises the freedom and the necessity to maintain the impossible possibility that love will achieve fulfilment. The impossibilities which we experience in, and which we contribute to, the ways of love are not to be dissolved away by reducing them to the products of our class consciousness and the alienations of our social structures. That theory, as well as producing important insights about the obstacles to love and the conditions required for loving, also produces its own contributions to the impossibilities and leaves the contradictions of love unresolved. Faith which is through Jesus Christ holds that there exists another way, which will ignore none of the impossibilities experienced or the contradictions produced but will find a way through them and beyond them because it is the way of the God who is the energy and the end of the universe. So the scope of the argument and the investigation on which we are engaged is all-embracing and it would be deeply irresponsible to the humanity of our fellows and of ourselves to bandy about arguments plucked from the air or taken up out of merely individual taste or choice.

Some account has therefore to be given of what it is that enables us, or even forces us, to pursue the argument in the way we are doing. This as I have already hinted, cannot compel the acceptance of the argument but it should expose the source of the argument and where it gets its strength from. The account should give some indication of what it is that sustains and directs the arguer in maintaining what he or she does maintain and what it is that pushes or beckons the explorer along the way which he or she feels obliged to investigate. In this way it may be possible to keep faith with our fellow human beings and seek to be a more genuine part of a common human exploration into truth and hope rather than an imposer of something one claims to possess. The account may also provide some reference to the possibilities of practice which are connected with developing the knowledge claimed and the hopes indicated. At least it must be made clear that we are concerned with a knowledge, a hope and a truth which cannot be gained from outside. It is a truth, a reality, which one finds oneself living out of and into.

Thus any account has to begin as an autobiographical confession which, as it develops, will seek to show how *my* knowing of God is part of what *we* (the believers) have known and are coming to know, as part of God's making himself known to *all*. The account has to make reference to God from the start because the basis for using language about truth, reality, ultimate hope, compulsion, guidance and so on is the conviction that God has made himself known to me. There is no claim that one has stumbled upon, been led to or succeeded in thinking out some all-embracing theory about the nature of the universe and the realities of being human. There is a claim to a knowing of God who establishes reality and who is committed to fulfilling the humanness of men and women.

This claim arises as a response to a reality experienced by myself and for myself but in the context of a community and of a continuing exploration of relationship. Thus I have to begin my 'giving of an account' which common respect for and responsibility to my fellow human beings requires, by stating that I find myself existing before God, within the church and in the continuing context of what is still best referred to as prayer. That is to say that I have some awareness of a presence around whom there is a community with a continuing tradition and in relation to whom there is the possibility of developing a living dependence and response. I have no other way of beginning my account because for me, living is before God and within God. That is to say as far as I can understand and feel about things, if there were no God there would be no life, if there were no God there would be no speaking, and if there were no God there would be no speaking of God. This is how I understand the realities in the midst of which I live and with which I am concerned. God and his outgoing existence and his outgoing making of himself known is the presupposition of living, speaking and speaking of him.

But secondly, knowing God and speaking of God is within the church. Experiences are kindled and language learnt and developed within a community. It is clear that neither biblically nor psychologically would people be able to speak of God and come to the knowledge of him if people did not already speak about God and have the knowledge of him.

The people of God, historically speaking and under God, are clearly an essential presupposition to being able to begin with God. (I would however hold that *all* people are in some sense 'people of God'. This however becomes recognizable and knowable because there are some particular people who have been *chosen* to be 'people of God' in the sense that they are the vehicles in history for this particular concrete knowledge of God's existence and of his attitude of love towards all men. It is not possible to develop here a discussion of the relationship between particular choice and general purpose but I hope that my starting from the contradiction of the tribalisms of Christianity and the general exploration of this book will be itself a contribution to this vital topic. One of the contradictions of Christianity has been the way in which Christians have made use of their particular calling to deny the universal purposes of God.)

Since in any account I give I have to attempt to speak of God who is the presupposition of my being and the context of all being, it is also clear that I can begin only from prayer. This is so because to know God is to know also that we are dependent upon him and called to a total commitment to him. Therefore we are committed to prayer as an attitude and disposition of response, of praise and of expectancy in relation to this God who is known and who promises so much more to be known. Further, the practice of prayer is necessary because to know God is to know also the inadequacy of our response to and readiness for both the relationship which he offers and the commitment which he requires. Therefore, something of the nature of prayer is a necessity and a natural concomitant of any practical knowledge of God. We are obliged, and also rejoice, to express our dependence and seek for a continuing repentance. This is to seek for new ways of thinking, of understanding and of acting which steadily become more appropriate to the immediacy of the knowledge of God and to the effect which this has and should have on our living and our relationship with everyone and everything in the world. I use the word 'prayer' therefore to refer to a whole range of activities, attitudes and dispositions which seek to respond to and develop an active awareness of the fact that we are 'living within' God and his purposes. Because of this 'living within' the reality of which I am seeking to give an account, and because of the corresponding way in which I am part of the argument and exploration which I am seeking to develop, it is clear that there is no other way to commence my account than to state that I find myself before God, within the church and in prayer.

Thus, in beginning to give my account I am obliged to start with an attempt, however jejune, to describe what forces me to attempt to be an artist who seeks to portray, however inadequately, the vision which he has glimpsed or the 'inside' of some aspect of reality to which he has penetrated. It is also like attempting to describe what motivates me to be a pilgrim, what guides me in the direction of the exploration which I am undertaking, or even what it is which prompts me to seek to be a lover. It may be held that artists, pilgrims, explorers and lovers are not good guides to reality but that what is required is something more like the 'hard facts' which are to be discovered much more 'scientifically'. About this men and women must make up their own minds, taking into account the widest possible range of facts and experiences known to them and making use of the widest possible range of insight, reflection and commitment that is available to them. All I am trying to do is make it quite clear that a claim to another kind of knowing is being made here and that it is being made obviously and deliberately. The depth and extent of that claim, and the fact that it is a claim to be in touch with reality in the deepest sense that that term can have, are made particularly clear by those who have come to be called the 'martyrs' of the Christian faith. They are those who judged it right, proper and appropriate to die rather than to deny or reject the God whom they had come to know and to serve. While I suspect that I should very probably fail to act as they did if I were placed in like circumstances, I am none the less quite clear that their choice and acts were epistemologically as well as morally correct, if I may so put it. They were simply being consistent with what they had learned about the reality of God, the world and themselves.

Thus it is a matter of experience to me which I must treat as amounting to knowledge that the basis of my living and the context of my living is God; that the sources of my most fundamental insights and hopes are found within the church (that is to say, within some form of Christian fellowship) and that there these insights are renewed, corrected and re-directed and developed; and that prayer as response, praise, expectancy, dependence, renewal and immediacy is something constant, however faltering. Thus I can also share, in however feeble and absurd a way, that 'I know' which is expressed explicitly in the gospel of St John and which is to be found in various ways in most of the New Testament documents. This 'I know' is perhaps best represented by that triumphant but teasing testimony at the end of the fourth gospel: 'It is this same disciple who attests what has here been written. It is in fact he who wrote it, and we know that his testimony is true' (John 21.24, NEB). Here we have an example of the way in which the authenticity of the testimony and knowledge is renewed again and again in the experience of the believing community. This role of community as a locus for knowledge will be discussed further later. Meanwhile and as a first step, I am seeking to draw attention to the nature of this experience and thus to the claim that it is an experience of knowing. Of course, I do not have the fullness of the experience which is witnessed to at the close of the fourth gospel, but I do have enough experience to glimpse what *that* definitive experience is about and hope that I shall learn more fully.

This part of my giving an account is thus an attempt to explain why my contradicted starting-point still remains my unquestionable starting-point. A vision, an insight, a knowledge and a love which are strong enough and deep enough are not overruled by contradictions but challenged by them. As I hope the exploration so far has strongly shown, the unquestionable starting-point within Christian faith and church is not an unquestioning starting-point, nor the starting-point of an enterprise which seeks to avoid questioning. Indeed my claim and conviction is quite the contrary. I believe that to know God is to be free to question everything. I further believe that to know God is to be bound to question anything. I do not exercise this freedom nor respond to this obligation very effectively because I am not yet really developed or practised in the knowledge of God. But I see sufficient to wish to depend upon God himself for this development, practice and growth in the questioning. And I know sufficient to hope that the growth in and the practice of such questioning and such freedom is a real possibility for me and for my fellow men and women.

Thus I believe that giving an account of the starting-point is part of the process of opening up the knowledge claimed, and setting it out for discussion, for the questioning which rises from the mind, the heart and the will. But while the knowledge is thus opened up for discussion, it still remains the basis on which one moves in the explaining, the exploring and the questioning. This is why the very contradiction of the Christian gospel and the Christian church has been examined on the basis of Christian knowledge and Christian insights. This also is why the discussion of the basis for Christian insights and Christian symbols is pursued in the middle of an exploration which is constantly using those insights and symbols. The basis for the exploration and the claims for the knowing are discoverable in the course of the exploration and in the search for the knowledge, the implications and applications. To attempt to establish a basis of knowledge by discussion before moving into the exploration would be impossible. Such an undertaking would both misrepresent and sterilize the position with regard to finding out what the human possibilities are and what the pilgrimage is about. The sort

of knowledge which needs to establish itself before it goes into action
will never do so. For how can faith or knowledge be built up save in
action and exploration and life ? Moreover true faith and living knowledge have built into them experienced elements of value, excitement
and command. They *must* be tried out, lived into, put into practice and
so be put to the test. Of course, by experiment and practice all may be
lost or at least all may be seen to be lost. As I have already written,
'Vision, faith and hope are not capable of having their true fullness and
reality decisively demonstrated. They can only be demonstrated and
pursued to authentication or to destruction' (p. 63), but I believe that it
is the inherent nature of true faith and living knowledge to suggest that
all is to be found. At least it seems clear that the questioning cannot
come before we seek to live things out but simply in living things out.

This attempt at explanation may also serve to bring it out into the
open that we are in fact engaged in a discussion and decision about how
we know and about how we find out what there is to be found out. For
the experience of faith is that there is the greatest possible connection
between how God is known and what he is known to be. Indeed, as far
as we are concerned the how of God's being known and the what he is
known to be are identical. That is to say that God is known in his acting,
his giving and his loving and that he is known to be act, gift and love.
This means that in any investigation into the knowledge of God and
what this offers to our humanity, it has constantly to be borne in mind
that 'I' (any participating self that is) and all men are part of the argument and that not merely conceptually but existentially. For the
knowledge of God arises because of the outgoing existence and love of
God whose very being and energy reaches out in creation and redemption, first of all to give being to everything else and then to incorporate
that which has self-conscious and responsive existence (among which
human beings are included) into God's own life and love. Hence any
attempt to investigate into and reflect on the reality and possibilities
which are offered to us for being human is an attempt to come to grips
with 'that in which we live and move and have our being', and that in a
twofold sense. We are concerned both with the very basis, condition or
ground of our existing at all and with that which fulfils our existence,
that is gives it a meaning and an enjoyment which is wholly satisfying
and self-evident.

Since we are 'part of the argument', it is inevitable in any exposition
to start 'in the middle', or in the midst, as we have found. That is to say
that there is no independent, objective or *a priori* established starting-
point for deciding who we are, what the world is about, or what it is or

might be to be human. We cannot argue about living from outside the argument. The question is 'Where do we find ourselves ?' Those who find themselves with a knowledge of God 'through Jesus' and among those who are called to worship God are obliged to attempt to live with the knowledge they so far have, in the light of the developing knowledge which this attempt and response brings them and for the sake of the total human enterprise of which they are part.

So far I have had to attempt to give my account of the grounds and shape of the hope that is in us by starting from an autobiographical account of knowledge of God. But as I indicated earlier in this chapter, the account should proceed by showing how '*my* knowing of God is part of what *we* (the believers) have known and are coming to know, as part of God's making himself known to *all*'. I want to consider more fully the claim about corporate knowing which is referred to briefly in chapter 2 and is a most important part of the claim that the knowledge which is reflected in the insights and symbols of Christian belief is in fact knowledge about reality.

The objectivity and givenness of this corporate knowledge, has, I believe, to be rehabilitated. It arises from experience and it is reflected back into the experience, even though the methods and modes of expressing it are often markedly mythological. The essentiality of corporate community knowledge and experience has tended to be greatly neglected or discouraged in Western Christian tradition and especially in modern Protestantism. As a result there has been an almost total disintegration of confidence in corporate knowledge, reflected not least in what has become a solely analytical and individualistic study of the Bible. This has been compounded by the mistake of assuming that we *know better* than they, that is to say than our predecessors in the Christian faith, rather than the more realistic situation which is that we tend to have a different understanding of knowledge from them. This promotion of our way of knowing to the status of a completely normative way is one more example of the tribalism which afflicts us and of the tendency to absolutize both our particular period of history and our particular culture within that period of history. We need to return therefore to a careful reconsideration of corporate and traditional knowing and of serious claims to direct awareness, given of course under differing cultural and conditioned forms, of the Mystery within which, from which and to which we might live. The over-exaltation of a narrowly intellectualistic way of knowledge leads us to ignore a way of knowing which arises from an interpenetration of reality and experience which is both intellectual and emotional and associated with a way of life and worship. Thus, even within Christian circles, we have tended to cease to believe or behave as if the pattern and regularity of praying and worshipping provides any guidance as to what is and should be believed about the reality to be encountered and the possibilities to be looked for. That is to say, '*Lex orandi lex credendi*' has ceased to be significant for us. I am convinced however that this needs to be strongly revived, along with all the help which can be obtained from Christian traditions which have never been individualized in this way and from cultures other than the Western which have never succumbed to the narrow views of epistemology and of the world which at any rate until recently have been dominant in the West.

Orthodoxy (right belief, right worship and the appropriate response to the glory which is glimpsed) and orthopraxy (the response in discipleship, both personal and social, to what is glimpsed in and as orthodoxy) have to be reinstated to their full place in elucidating the significance for reality and for being human of the experience of the worshipping and witnessing community through the ages and across the world. Thus God is known to be God because he establishes himself as God in the experience, response and tradition of those who understand themselves, their hopes and the world in relation to him. We must not drive a wedge between God, stories about him and the people who told the stories. Nor must we forget that the stories reflect experience of him among the people in whom he becomes known and are designed to be used as part of the renewal of this experience among these people and those who will join them. It is from this continuing reservoir of renewed and renewable experience that there arises the claim for objectivity of the knowledge of God or, certainly, for the objectivity of the God who is known and the givenness of knowledge about him. This givenness comes alive as it is reflected in and experienced as his 'giving-ness' in the current situations and experiences of believers. Of course, if there is no association whatever with a believing community and a total rejection of the credibility and reliability of all believing communities, then all sorts of explanations and explainings away are to be expected and will seem entirely proper. Without some share in the essential experience of dependence upon and worship of God in a community there is no sustaining basis for knowing him or believing that such knowledge exists. There will be no demanding base for claiming that he is, still less a basis for believing that there is any knowledge available about who he is.

The effects of separating any talk of or assessment of knowledge from necessary association with a believing community, a personal spirtuality and a sustained attempt to work out appropriate patterns of response is to be seen in the destructive effects of analytic and scientific biblical criticism where that is taken as being wholly and solely normative of what is to be believed and what can be known. (I hope that my insistence elsewhere and in other contexts on taking history seriously will be sufficient to allow me to simply interpolate here that I do not wish by the argument which I am at present following to question the proper validity of these scientific methods of biblical criticism. I believe that they are a necessary part of taking the revelation of God in history seriously and that there are many creative and important critical effects of this activity. Consequently I am not calling it in question as a general procedure with its own particular uses but at the moment simply arguing about its normative value concerning faith and knowledge.) By allowing a particular type of criticism to take on a normative value, we have driven an immense wedge between, first, God (who becomes 'God', that is, a mere concept or language-object) and, secondly, the stories about him and the people who told the stories and lived by the stories and, thirdly, the assessing intellects about what is really true, what might really have happened and what may be truly believed. The first and second of these three separate items or areas of knowledge and experience are then evaluated from the assumed standpoint of the third. After this, since most of those who bother to go in for this sort of exercise do so from some Christian commitment, some attempt is then made to put some fragments together again and regain some sense of wholeness or possibility of belonging by an effort, very often solipsistic and almost always individualistic, to restore an existential awareness of 'being' or of 'God'. But one clearly cannot escape into a wider experience of either corporate belief or corporate behaviour from an individualistic intellect curved in upon itself by taking an extra twist a little more deeply into the same isolated intellect and experience.

This breaking up of an organic and dynamic whole seems to lead inevitably to reductionism in the sense that practically the whole body of material which is found in the Bible and in the tradition of the church is held to be *only* church talk or *only* the culturally conditioned mythical account of a faith experience. This tends to become fatal for the relationship of faith to reality, because it prevents the talk or the myths from being understood as reflecting, in their own way, experiences of an objectively existing Mystery with which we are involved and of which we are a part. Thus any possibility of a claim about an actually transcendent God who can make his own way against or beyond the events and resources of history disappears. Accounts have to be given of Christian faith, tradition and doctrine which are within what is alleged to be the permanent and all-conquering 'spirit of the age'. We are left also with an approach which despises and ignores the human experience of the believing community from whenever it emerged into history after Abraham until, say, the time of Schleiermacher. It also ignores the experience of all those cultures which have not yet been 'modernized' on the common ground that our way of knowing must be better, that is to say, that this way of knowing is more consistent with reality than any of these other ways of perception and experience. Thus our Christianity in the West has tended to add to its own contradiction by dissolving away any sense of a living and powerful God of whom it could be said in any truthful or realistic way that he both transcends and confronts actual and continuing contradictions.

We are, however, able to return to the possibilities and trends of corporate and traditional knowing and also to the possibilities and trends of direct awareness of the Mystery who is the transcendent God. As a way of taking slightly further what is implied here, I should like to make use of an article by an Indian theologian[1] which sets out in very short compass, with the help of certain Sanskrit concepts, an account of corporate Christian knowing which is, I believe, much more consistent with giving an explanation for the grounds and shape of the hope that is in us. Its purpose, as its title suggests, is to reflect on the ways in which one could move from more traditional Christologies to something more appropriate to Indian ways of thinking. This is clearly a highly important subject in itself but not one which can be pursued here. I am venturing to make use of the following quotations from this article because they reflect on the general issue of our objective knowledge of realities through and in the Christian tradition.

He first defines anubhava as follows:

The word *anubhava* in the Hindu religio-philosophical tradition literally means 'to be in fellowship with concrete realities'. In content it is man's realization of the Bhavavastha, the existential dimension of reality in its encounter with man. In English the word which approximately carries this meaning may be 'experience'. In concrete terms, anubhava implies a cumulative awareness of the Reality in the sentiment, intellectual and intuitive spheres of man. Among these spheres there is real psychological overlapping and osmosis of consciousness; they give man a concrete and unique content of anubhava as he encounters Reality. It is

[1] T. M. Manickam, 'Anubhava as Pramana of an Indian Christology', *Jeevadhara: a Journal of Christian Interpretation* (published from the Theology Centre, Alleppey, Kerala, India), vol. 1, no. 3, 1971, pp. 228 f.

with this fuller and deeper meaning that we use the term anubhava as denoting the person-to-person experience of man with Christ in the Indian context.

He then describes pramana:

The world *pramana* means 'source' or means of information. It implies also 'criterion' by which to measure the progress of an action. It is dynamic in that it takes on new meaning and new dimensions as the action develops. Action contributes to experience, and one unit of experience serves as the pramana for the next unit of action. It is here that we see the interrelation of anubhava and pramana contributing and interacting mutually. Through this interaction, anubhava is perfected with the characteristic elements it receives from the past and present stages of action, and is open to its future. Action here is the encounter with Christ of numberless men of every age and culture. This encounter which constitutes anubhava becomes, therefore, the source and criterion (pramana) of further anubhava.

He then applies this to Christology as follows:

The starting point of Christology is the Christ-event, the life, suffering, death and resurrection of Christ as experienced by his disciples. This experience was grace-bearing and effective of salvation. But the grace and salvation were clothed in the socio-cultural expressions drawn from the background of the apostles. The grace-giving experience of the Christ-event was communicated to other communities of men down the ages through the preaching of the apostles, their writings, and especially the sacramental action of the Church. In all, the grace-bearing contact with the Christ-event through anubhava constituted the core of Christology, and the cultural expressions that communicated the anubhava were its vehicle. These cultural expressions had a flexible character and varied greatly from age to age and from culture to culture. The function of theology is to interpret and explain the actual transmission of this saving Christ-event as presented in Scripture, in the traditions of the churches and the official declaration of the Church. Though the early Church emphasised in its theology the centrality of anubhava in the contact with Christ, later theologians took this internal element for granted and neglected it. In a great number of theological manuals Christ is interpreted in terms of ancient documents without sufficiently stressing the fact that these documents merely recorded the Christ-anubhava, preserved and communicated in a living manner through the activity of the Church.

The above, I believe, outlines one very effective way of presenting the Christian claim to knowledge about divine and human reality. Christianity is fundamentally and ultimately an anubhava, an experience of the divine in Jesus Christ and all that follows from and contributes to this. The starting-point in history of this particular knowledge of the divine in relation to the human is the primitive Christian community which experienced Jesus as a divine intervention in history for human salvation. This experience is re-enjoyed, re-conveyed and further explored by the continuing community and communities in each of the situations in which they find themselves. This experience and exploration is carried out with the help of reference to the recorded anubhava in the New Testament, by the experience of life and worship in the community and through mutual accountability between the various Christian communities, and there is also a building up of a knowledge about God and man by systematic reflection in relation to the totality of human experience. I would add that this last element is as central as the other two. Any tendency to dwell solely within the original experience and solely within the internal life of the community will deprive the community and its members of an essential element in any living knowledge of God. This is because the forms in which the original record is stated and the forms which are to be found in the internal life of the community of believers, while they were originally a response to the living reality of the living God, may not now reflect the reality under the conditions of present times, and certainly may not now convey this reality or put people now onto this reality. Hence it is essential that the records and the life of the community should be submitted to both the provocation and the check of what is going on in the world. The knowledge of God includes the knowledge that he is at work in the whole world and that he is concerned with responding to and fulfilling the needs and possibilities of all men and all women. This is why it is appropriate to place a discussion about the living God and the reality of the hope that is in us in the midst of a discussion about the contradictions, possibilities and needs of human living today.

Thus my knowledge of God is part of our knowledge of God which has to be extended, corrected and developed in relation to the world as a whole. The heart of this claim to knowledge is probably pointed to as clearly as anywhere in the words attributed to Jesus in the Gospel according to St John: 'The teaching that I give is not my own; it is the teaching of him who sent me. Whosoever has the will to do the will of God shall know whether my teaching comes from him or is merely my own' (John 7. 16 f., NEB). The Authorized Version of part of this reads: 'If any man will do his will he shall know of the doctrine, whether it be of God, or whether I speak of myself.' But the New English Bible reflects the play on words in the Greek with its 'whoever has the *will* to do this *will* of God shall know'. The critical point is this connection between commitment and action on the one hand and knowledge on the other. The practice of response in the world and in life then builds up the knowledge that the 'doctrine' is not just what somebody says but reflects and points to God, his energies and his purposes. Thus the notion of interpenetration between reality and experience in a cumulative way building up and testing knowledge is central to the Christian claim for knowledge of God.

The idea is further given one of its clearest and, for us, most suggestive expressions in the notion of *theoria* as developed by the Greek Fathers. The notion comes from the Platonic tradition but is given a more practical and a more practising twist. Cornford in his book *From Religion to Philosophy* describes Theoria as 'passionate sympathetic contemplation'.[2] There are affinities here with the notion of anubhava referred to above. There is nothing cold or detached about real knowledge, that is to say about the knowledge of reality. In order to enter into this knowledge it is necessary to develop a sympathy and a commitment which brings about an interpenetration, a living within the realities and a living of the realities within, between the one who contemplates or receives the knowledge and the knowledge received. This is an intellectual vision which is associated with a way of life which is a necessary preparation to the vision and a necessary accompaniment to developing in the vision. For Christians this preparation and way of life involves the love of God and the love of man, that is to say, an attempt to enter into the life of Christ and to receive this life through and in the spirit. 'Passionate sympathetic' contemplation and practice does not simply enable a detached seeing of God or a series of remote glimpses which encourage the building up of hypotheses or mere guesses. It involves starting on a way which is a way of participation in God and with God. It is less like looking at an object and weighing up external evidence than like participating in a life, where the energizing power is that of God who proceeds beyond any images or evidence.

Of course, the knowledge is not a possession and the capacity to respond to the knowledge received and so grow in knowledge is, in most of us, only feeble. In any case, growth in such knowledge would involve some participation in all the struggles, contradictions and sufferings which are clearly part of God's commitment to the world and his energetic and passionate working for the fulfilment of all creative and human possibilities. Thus the knowledge cannot be a possession controlled by the knower nor something which can be shared with a

[2] F. M. Cornford, *From Religion to Philosophy. A Study in the Origins of Christian Speculation*, Edward Arnold 1912, p. 198.

simple and detached objectivity, regardless of the activities and commitments of the persons concerned. But where there is response, both individual and communal, there is the possibility of gaining the knowledge which has been communally and experientially built up and there is the opportunity of extending this knowledge and contributing the fruits of it to the common human struggle and hope. What is experienced, however faintly and with however many contradictions, is a way of life which is related to God's life. Contemplation, worship, prayer, exploration and action develop from and contribute to an active knowing. Thus one is obliged to bear witness to the Reality known and to seek ways of developing this response and knowledge in relation to all the current problems and possibilities of being human. Since one is confronted by what is one cannot but respond. Reality is not to be denied. Since this Reality offers a faith, a power and a possibility of love which gets into the contradictions which threaten human beings as possibilities of love, it is not obligation which controls the response but hope and praise.

Such then is the outline of an explanation for the grounds and shape of the hope that is in me and for the continuing use of Christian symbols and insights in the conflict and the search for being human. This account has forced itself into the middle of the exploration and argument because it has seemed necessary to indicate at least the beginning of ways of answering some such questions as the following. First, where do we get our grounds for facing the immense contradictions with which we are surrounded and for claiming transcendence of these contradictions in the very midst of them? Secondly, how do I give a responsible account to fellow human beings about the sort of claims and symbols that are being advanced with regard to being human? Sensitivity to and respect for our common human condition seems to make mere propaganda something very inhuman and unworthy. It is therefore necessary to try to make it clear to everyone, including us Christians ourselves, that Christianity claims to be a process of growing knowledge about reality. This may well heighten the contradictions. But claims are both felt and made about truth which make it necessary to combat things apparently contrary to this truth and make it necessary also that Christian faith and practice should be exposed to refutation and rejection if they cannot be maintained in worship, response and suffering. Since I am on to something of passionate importance and involved in writing about a concern for being human, it seems necessary at least to glance at the question of what right anyone has to urge these views and recommend this sort of exploration. On reflection it is clear to me that, in a sense, no one can have such a right. The sufferings and the possibilities of our fellow human beings are so great that, on the whole, to write about them and claim to respond to them threatens to be a monstrous imposition. But perhaps there could be and there is something like the right of an artist or of one following a vision, of a jester or of a lover. But in exercising such a right or presuming on such a liberty one would wish to combine resolute fidelity to what is offered, eagerness to share and an openness which might make sharing possible.

7

Image of God and kingdom of God

We return, then, to the main concern of our exploration. Granted that we authentically find ourselves involved in and committed to developing a way of life which is related to God's life, what is the bearing of Christian insights and symbols on our historical struggles to be human? The thrust for this exploration comes, as we have seen, from two dilemmas. The first dilemma comes to me as a white bourgeois English Christian but the second dilemma comes to me simply as a human being. The first is that I discover that my Western expression of Christianity contradicts that universal love and offer of God for which Christianity stands. My first dilemma is that I am involved in a Christianity which, in effect, denies Christ. Are Jesus Christ and his gospel therefore to be denied? The second dilemma, however, makes it all the more imperative that Jesus Christ and his gospel should not be denied. For this second dilemma is the universal human dilemma of the contradiction of love. The humanity of man is contradicted by his inhumanity. Yet the gospel vision is a vision of love at work to fulfil the glimpsed glory of being human in a manner which does full justice to the glories only glimpsed and the love often contradicted. Can it be therefore that the gospel is truly and sufficiently good news about human being and becoming because it points to possibilities and resources for measuring up to the repeated denials both of the gospel and of humanity with which history and our present experience confronts us? To be gospel indeed this gospel must point to power to confront that which contradicts it and especially that which contradicts it in history through those who profess, proclaim and promote it.

To have any hope of facing this question and of discerning a gospel which goes deep enough into human and historical contradictions and threats to be realistically hopeful, we find that we have to face the age-old and universal question, which the Greeks put in succinct form: '*Pothen to kakon*?' (that is, where does what is bad come from?) What clues do the symbols and insights of Christian experience offer us here?

As a Christian, that is, one who takes the Bible seriously and as revealing decisive indications concerning God's dealing with man, my argument is that the Marxists point us to clues which are particularly appropriate to our present historical condition. We are given an understanding of the way in which the poor and the oppressed are decisive indications of what is wrong with our present human societies. As part of this demonstration, and this is *most* important, we are shown how our own involvement in these societies distorts and limits our own understandings of what is wrong and what should or could be done about it.

However, an examination of Marxist theory carried out together with some consideration of the biblical understanding of the poor and with some survey of human possibilities as we experience them leads us also to challenge Marxism very seriously. Taken as a whole, and as whole which is claimed to be a total explanation, the Marxist answer to 'Where does what is bad come from?' is both false and dehumanizing. Further, discussion in this areas shows, as was indicated at the end of chapter 5, that the way we answer the question 'What is wrong with the human situation?' is a function of what we hold to be *right* and *true* about the human situation. Your diagnosis of evil reflects your hopes and beliefs about the realities and the possibilities of good.

In accordance with this insight I have argued that to see men and women as held together in solidarity in sin is part of both a more hopeful and a more glorious view of man than to see them as locked together in nothing but class conflict and structures of exploitation. Moreover such a view frees us for a much wider appreciation of a wider range of human possibilities and experiences than is open on the Marxist interpretation. By confining men to history and to history interpreted in the peculiarly Marxist way, Marxism reduces men and women to something much less than their truly human stature and future.

But this type of discussion, which is a discussion about the real nature of things and about the energies which are truly at work in the universe and in man, makes clear that we are in the realm of faith and of vision as well as that of attempting to respond to unpleasant discoveries and deal with urgent practical and political questions. This is why it became necessary, in the middle of the discussion, to insert an attempt to describe the sort of things which give Christian faith and vision weight and authenticity as motivating and guiding forces in the struggle to be human. It has to be made clear that in facing up to urgent practical necessities, making diagnoses of 'what is wrong' and seeking to put into practice measures to 'put things right', I am automatically concerned, either explicitly or implicitly, with beliefs about the future of man and about what it means to be human. Basically, therefore, I am not primarily concerned to solve a problem but to pursue a vision – and to consider the vision's meaning both in hope and in action. Hence, as I am a Christian I have to explore into what it means to be a Christian, at this place of cultural and racial space and at this point of historical time. I have further to ask how the particular realities relate to the universal possibilities. But this, of course, depends on what I believe to be the universal possibilities which are offered. It is my conviction that these possibilities are transcendent, that they are, indeed, the possibilities of the transcendent God himself and that it is these possibilities which are opened to us by the Transcendent in our midst. The full development and the filling full of these possibilities lies in the future. That is why we know so little in detail, have to work out everything in practice and need again and again to be jolted by such as Marxists out of the way in which we have idolized and sanctified real but temporary discoveries made in the past. For we are concerned with the future of the Transcendent, that is to say the future which the Transcendent God finally brings about and the future which consists in the enjoyment of the being and becoming of the Transcendent God, which is the being and becoming of love. So we need constantly to be rescued from our past and from the false idols which we have fashioned out of our past in order to be part of the moving and building towards this future. We have, however, also to insist on and bear witness to the fact that it is *this* future, i.e. the future of God, which alone 'defines' men and women. Men and women need to be liberated from the inhumanities of a Christianity and a Christendom which have played their part in distorting the future of the kingdom of God into the past and present tyrannies of moral and political ideologies and structures. Men and women need also to be liberated from the inhumanities liable to be developed by political and social practices which see them as defined by their present roles in the historical process and by their apparent contribution to a mythical classless society. Our vision of the future and our forms of commitment to this vision are critical with regard to our contribution to the present struggles over the inhumanities of man to man.

But what does this concern about the reality of the vision of the future mean and how might it have meaning ? We need to consider the vision before we come to the response, to look into the 'theory' before we come to the practice. It is perhaps, necessary to dwell on this and to ask for patience here because so many people seem to be both terrifyingly and tiresomely hooked by the demand for instant relevance and immediate practicality whereas it is, in fact, and in practice, the dreadful impracticality of the practical man which is both the expression and the source of so much that is dehumanizing in our technological, commercial societies and in our revolutionary activities. Take, for example, the situation at the time of the general election, 1974, when the lectures out of which this book has been developed were being given. Everybody knew (all the leaders in all the leading papers, with the exception of the *Morning Star*, said so) that our trouble was inflation. This must be dealt with either by controlling wages or by stabilizing prices or by a judicious combination of such policies together with taxation and control of the money supply. It would be impracticable in so serious and acute a crisis to raise theoretical questions about, for example, justice and injustice or about more equal participation in the exercise of power. Moreover, questions of *that* sort might easily encourage 'extremists' and be politically divisive when unity was required to face the 'real' issues. Hence the political debate about how, in the mid 70s, we move towards the 80s was reduced to terms deriving largely from the 30s and an editorial of a leading Sunday paper (entitled 'Inflation – How the parties compare') was reduced to ending: 'Voters will simply have to pick and choose, sparing a thought for both parties' record in office – and then hope for the best.' There could scarcely be a more striking example of the way we are reduced to ineffective banality 'where there is no vision'.

Further examples of impractical practicality and irrelevant relevance can too easily be found in, for example, investigating what is held to be practical and relevant in the running of a hospital complex. 'Practical' means what is required in practice to keep the present practice going and relevant means what is relevant to the demands and requirements of the practitioners as they at present understand themselves. No account can be taken of any evidence or questioning which suggests that a great hospital complex has many features which are more disease-producing than health-promoting. (Of course, this formulation depends a great deal on what you mean by 'health', and that is a theoretical question.) Or again, we are faced with the practical needs and aims of a commercial and industrial process which is geared to creating needs so that they can be met by ever-increasing production in a world whose limits are ever becoming more obvious, But, as I have often been told, the basic responsibility of management remains 'to make a profit' and it is into that practical demand that the relevance of social or ecological responsibility has to be subsumed.

On the other hand, we all know that the dreadful impracticality of the practical man is well matched by the nauseating irrelevance of the theoretical man. But here we are faced with the dehumanizing diminution of the very word and notion of 'theory' and its derivative adjective 'theoretical'. Theory is something which is subservient to practice and 'theoretical' refers to that which is abstract and remote from the affairs with which men normally have to deal and through which they work out whatever destiny they have. It is implied that men and women do not have dealings and destinies which go beyond or might go beyond the practical, the immediate and the phenomenal. The possibility of eternal depth or infinite dimension is excluded from the imagination before any discussion is entered into of what is theoretical, what is practical and what are possible relationships between them. We need, therefore, a considerable disturbance of the ways of thinking and reacting which we are customarily conditioned to follow and all the reinforcing help we can get if we are to stand up against the pressures of the so-called practical. It requires a real effort and some hopeful boldness once again to look into, and to look out for, dimensions of human living and possibilities of human becoming which may transform our present understandings of what is practical and relevant in the direction of transcendent life and transcendent love.

It is my contention that we who are Christians are particularly encouraged to do this by the discovery that our two dilemmas converge together. The contradiction of Christ by expressions of Christianity and the contradictions of love by the expressions of man's inhumanity to man both converge together on the one problem and threat of what, in chapter 1, I called the pathology of our human identity. In considering the experience and effects of our tribalisms I then pointed out that 'that by which we identify ourselves and have our sense of identity, significance and belonging is also that by which we dehumanize others' (see p. 16). For example, human being and becoming is distinguished by the capacity for scientific discovery and then for technological application. Yet it is these very identifying traits of humanity and especially of Western men which have produced means and effects of both domination and distortion which threaten human existence and reduce many to a dehumanized and exploited life.

Or again, freedom, the liberty to partake in the shaping of their own lives and destinies, is something which men and women claim and fight for as essential to their identity as human beings. Yet many use their freedom to dominate or ignore other men or to treat women as less than human, while the fight for freedom does violence in its course and often produces authoritarian ideologies who deny freedom except in a pattern which they dogmatically define – and which is therefore bondage for some, if not for many.

Or again, language is one of the most distinctive characteristics of human being. The elaborate, deep and rich communication which language makes possible is essential to any truly human existence and is, perhaps one of the chief signs and tools of human transcendence in space and time over space and time. Yet language is a great source of rejection, dominance and non-communication. Those who do not speak 'our language' are inferior human beings, if human at all. Listening, like speaking must be done on our terms. The language of conquerors invades, dominates and distorts the language and culture of the conquered. Violence is liable to be done daily in international organizations by the insensitive use of the English language and of Anglo-Saxon methods and procedures in dealings with persons of other mother tongues.

Thus *we are faced not only with a Christianity in caricature but also with a humanity in caricature*. Yet it is no use simply fixing on some aspect or aspects of the distortions in the caricature and declaring that they are the causes which, if corrected, will enable the caricature of human being to be changed into its true image. For how can one tell what are the decisive causes and what are the incidental symptoms in the contradicted and contradicting behaviour and becoming of human beings? One cannot understand the significance and bearing of a caricature or a distortion without a previous understanding of the true image. This is another way of approaching the point which I have already made to the effect that the way we understand what is wrong with man indicates what we believe to be right and true about him.

Hence, our approaches to men and women and to their contradictions and possibilities are bound to imply and to express our *theory* about what it is or might be to be human. If we insist on being, as we call it, 'pragmatic' (or 'matter-of-fact') and refuse deeper reflection, disturbance or exploration, then we are bound to be treating human beings as simply 'things', that is as nothing but an interesting collection of the *pragmata* from which the adjective 'pragmatic' derives. But human beings are not things, they are persons. And in the Christian vision and understanding they are not even just historical persons (although they are at least that) they are potentially *eternal persons*.

For the Christians understanding of that humanity of ours which is now so often a humanity in caricature derives from a clear image of the humanity which is at present caricatured, disturbed or only partially expressed. This is the image which Christians believe to have been endorsed and embodied in history by Jesus and it is the *image of God* –

and nothing less. This, then, is the Christian theory of human being and becoming, that man is in the image of God. It is from this theory that the understanding of man as sinner, as one who falls short of the glory of God, arises. Thus talk about sin is not purely empirical talk. It is talk about a whole range of empirical phenomena to do with contradicting and contradictoriness, placing these phenomena in a certain theoretical context, the context of understanding man as created in the image of God.

We are not, however, dealing here with a 'mere theory' in that diminished sense of theory to which I referred earlier, as an abstraction built up, in a fragile way, out of practices and experiments, or as a speculation to be discussed in no very clear relation to actual living and loving. The sense of 'theory' which is involved here is something much more akin to the significance which the original word *theoria* had for the Greeks of the early centuries of the church, and to which I have already referred in the previous chapter (p. 91). It is related to a practical and practising insight into a living mystery. For *theoria* was used, and needs to be revived, to refer to the spiritual capacity to develop insight into the vision and action of God, both beyond all things and through all things. This capacity is developed and deepened by the grace of God received through fellowship and the discipline of prayer, worship and a sustained pursuit of Christian discipleship in all things. Indeed, the spiritual capacity to see into and respond to the very heart and energy of things is the expression and experience of being in the image of God. It is because men and women are created by God in the image of God that they have the capacity to see and respond to him and to his energetic activities and possibilities in one another, in themselves and in all things.

This 'creation by God in the image of God' does not mean that men and women are, as it were, turned off a divine production line ready-made with all the necessary sensors and feed-back mechanisms which will enable them to 'home-in' on God. It means something which is at once far more fragile and far more tough, far more tentative and far more flexible, far more risky and far more free. The reference to creation and to image is reference to a given potentiality, an opportunity and a power, to respond to living and loving relationships and so develop in the image of the God, response to whom is a possibility. Thus the idea of being and becoming in the image of God cannot possibly be a mere theory. It either involves practice, prayer and exploration, all of which are to do with the development of *theoria*, or it is reduced to mere fantasy and the flatulence of words.

The challenge, then, of maintaining that human being and becoming is to be understood within the theory of man as in the image of God is the challenge of practice, response and hope. What is it to live out the theory of being in the image of God and what is it to live out of the resources implied by or required by that theory ?

Here I want to return to what I referred to in chapter 2 as 'two very useful tools for our investigation' into the mutual interrelation between Christian identity and human identity (p. 26) These are the two concepts of *relationship* and *community*. I believe that these two concepts can and should be understood as pointing to what is essentially involved in being and becoming human and in the building up and fulfilling of both Christian and human identity. The lines along which the Christian 'theory' of man should be understood can be briefly indicated as follows. We can then go on to consider the implications of this for both understanding and action in the closing chapters.

In chapter 2 I offered a formulation which stated that 'men and women are that which their relationships enable them to become' (p. 26). This is, I think, in accordance with both Christian theory and Marxist theory. The essential difference lies in the relationships which are believed to be available. Relationships are what are constitutive of our being and of our identity. We do not *have* identity as an objective thing. Indeed, we are not objective beings. 'I' am not an object but a recognizably continuing pattern of events, relationships and responses, a continuing pattern which is self-conscious and, as such, self-affecting. (I can have relationships with and responses to myself, as well as to things and beings 'not myself.') Thus 'I' or any human being am a process, extended through time, with a continuing but changing personal pattern consisting of an immensely complex series of events which include relationships and responses. The basis of this pattern, in historical time, is my *body* (which, incidentally, is itself, as we now know, a process maintaining a recognizable but changing pattern). But the personal pattern who is 'I' is not to be identified with my body. It is to be found in the self-conscious responsive pattern which enjoys, sustains and suffers from 'my' relationships. It is precisely because these relationships include relationships with the God involved in history and nature but who transcends history and nature that 'I' and all human beings are not confined to history and nature. The transcendent possibilities which we know or can know in relationships are the image in us of the Transcendent Reality and energy who is God. The transcendent possibilities in us are the image of God responding to that image in others and all reflecting, and responding to, the Transcendent Reality into whose image we are developing.

But this process of the growth of the image out of the potentialities of the image towards the fullness of him who is imaged is not an *individual* process. Indeed, I am increasingly of the view that 'the individual' is a myth and a dangerously dehumanizing myth. We are not individuals, we are persons. (The only totally individual thing about us would be a dead body as distinct from a living and conscious one.) The process of the development of the potentialities of the image of God which is the process of being and becoming human is the process of the development of *community*. Relationships require and imply community. But a truly human community is not a collective. It must be a pattern of mutual relationships which both permits and enables each of the persons involved to exercise and enjoy the fulfilment of their relationships in a manner which permits and enables the same fulfilment for all. *We cannot be human until all are human.*

But it is precisely this type of community which is lacking and has been lacking throughout history. What we actually have are tribalisms which confine the exercise of being human to limited and selected parts of human kind, together with oppression and exploitation (overt or covert, acknowledged and deliberate or unrealized and condoned by default) which make the many humanly marginal in the interests of the few, whose humanity is distorted by the conditions of their privilege and power. Hence there can be no realistic talk of a theory of men and women as in the image of God nor any hopeful talk of the unity and fulfilment of human kind unless there is some prospect of a community which fulfils and some foretaste of that community in the here and now of present human existence.

The Marxist myth of a classless society in the historical future is an understandable projection of a necessary ideal if one hopes for truly human fulfilment. But it is a desperate myth, for it points only to something no living person will enjoy and it hopes for a historical reality which must contradict all the contradictions of history.

For the Christian, the theory and practice of man in the image of God is complemented by the experience and hope of the power and the future of the kingdom of God. This is the biblical, pictorial and poetic way of referring to our understanding that the energy and activity of God which is at work in the world is the energy and activity which constitutes the pattern of the final future.

The basis, the energy and the fulfilment of all relationships is love. This is so because God is love and God is the basis, the energy and the fulfilment of all things. He is working, therefore, to 'establish his kingdom', that is the community where all relationships are fulfilled and fulfilling. The power of this kingdom is precisely the same energy and reality as that which is expressed in and as perfect and perfecting community – namely the power and energy of invincible and uninterrupted love.

Thus both image of God and kingdom of God are references to relationships, energies and realities which are at work now and mutually complementing one another to establish in the end a pattern of fulfilment which takes up and maintains all the potentialities of love in a system of dynamic and mutually fulfilling relationships. God establishes man in a divine-human collaboration which releases all the energies of human being in a co-operation with, and enjoyment of, all the glory of the energy of the divine. *The ultimate future and fulfilment of being human lies neither in revolution nor in extinction but in transfiguration.*

But the historical truth and promise of this human fulfilment beyond history is pointed to and authenticated by Jesus Christ, his cross and his resurrection. It is Jesus, fulfilled in his cross and resurrection, who is the historical embodiment and decisive symbol of Transcendence in the midst and it is Jesus in his cross and resurrection who points to the working pattern of Transcendence in the midst of all history and all human being and becoming. It is with this clue, the clue of the crucified Christ, that we must go on from our theory of man as indicated by image of God and kingdom of God to consider the practice of hope, of faith and of love which is offered to us and required of us in history and for being human.

8

Radical spirituality and radical politics

We come now, therefore, to questions about the practice of Transcendence in the midst or to questions about those practices which are appropriate for responding to and exploring into Transcendence in the midst. The phrase 'radical spirituality and radical politics' used as a general way of describing this practice reflects a theory concerning God, man and world, in the sense of theory discussed in the last chapter. That is to say, it is concerned with a vision and understanding of what is involved in human being and becoming. It is concerned with the context, the possibilities and the hopes which are held to be actually existent for men and women. Thus, my argument and hope is that I am developing a Christian theory about this and that therefore what I have now to discuss is patterns or hints of Christian discipleship. For this, in my theory, that is in my understanding and vision of the Christian revelation, is about how you should live towards Christian identity and towards human identity, towards Christian unity and community and towards human unity and community. For ultimately, as I explain more fully in chapter 10, they are one and the same and neither are fulfilled until both are fulfilled. The connection between Christian identity and human identity is very well expressed in the following sentence: 'You do not become a man in order to become a Christian; you become a Christian in order to become a man.' I know that this is a sentence which has been put to me as a quotation in conversation but I cannot, alas, remember who made this point to me, so that I cannot trace the source of the quotation. None the less it seems to me to put very clearly a fundamental point about our Christian discipleship, our commitment to God in Jesus Christ and our commitment to being and becoming human. Thus the whole point of arguing against certain features of Marxism or certain aspects, say, of the so-called 'theology of liberation' is that they are not human enough. It is not desired or intended to argue that they are 'not Christian enough'. As I have already said, our fundamental concern is not with being either Christian or Marxist but with being human. I am arguing however that it is from our Christian tradition, illuminated and enlivened by modern pressures and judgments, that we can be made sensitive to perceive the 'not human enough'. Thus it should be our Christian theory and vision sensitively understood which alerts us to the possibilities of the tragedy of sin and the way that these possibilities involve also the heroes and leaders of revolution and of creative newness. Our theory and faith also enable us to recognize, evaluate for what it is fully worth, and celebrate the glory of human achievements despite sin and in the midst of sinful structures which we know also need to be changed. Further we are set free fully to enjoy the foretaste now of being human which is possible in the immediacy of human relationships because of the ever-present Spirit of God who is also fighting with us against all that is contrary to being human and to strengthen all that is already present of the creative possibilities of being human. All this should keep us alert to detect and cherish every evidence of the glory of eternity and of universality which is potentially present in each and every human being, no matter what their present social state or condition. For it is this eternity and universality which is offered to every 'I' who is in the image of God. We are not 'individuals'; we are persons, as I pointed out in the previous chapter. But each of us is a 'named person', a personal pattern of relationships designed for fulfilment in our own personal pattern within the whole pattern which is offered to us by God. Again, this will be taken up further in the last chapter. Just now I am simply concerned to indicate the grounds on which we are bound to seek to criticize and attack anything that turns out to be 'not human enough'.

This protest and criticism on behalf of the 'not human enough' must however be both forward-looking and realistic if it is not to permit and promote fantasy, defensiveness, hypocrisy and repression. We are back here to our whole problem of the contradiction of Christianity. We must, therefore, interpret and practice our theory in a forward-looking way. We are concerned with the developing of humanity and of humanness 'towards one new man in Christ Jesus'. We are not concerned with the imposing of any patterns of being human which we have so far received and practised, no matter how much we may cherish them. Indeed, we are concerned to grow out of our patterns so far and beyond them into the newness wherein the full possibilities of being human will be fully fulfilled. It is in this connection of not imposing patterns hitherto accepted and of escaping from the distortions of patterns which are still around that we are required also to be strictly and sufferingly realistic. To encourage us in this realism I reproduce the famous passage in which Marx exposes what he believes to be the true nature of religion in its relation to being and becoming human.

> The misery of religion is at once an expression of and a protest against real misery. Religion is the sigh of the oppressed creature, the sentiment of a heartless world and the soul of soulless conditions. It is the opium of the people. The abolition of religion, which is the illusory happiness of men, is a demand for real happiness. The call to abandon their illusions about their condition is a call to abandon a condition which requires illusions. The criticism of religion is, therefore, the embryonic criticism of this vale of tears of which religion is the halo. Criticism has plucked the imaginary flowers from the chain, not in order that man shall bear the chain without the consolation of his fantasies but so that he shall cast off the chain and pluck the living flower. The criticism of religion disillusions man so that he will think, act and fashion his reality as a man who has lost his illusions and regained his reason; so that he will revolve about himself as his own true sun. Religion is only the illusory sun about which man revolves so long as he does not revolve about himself.[1]

Realism requires that we take full account of the unhappiness of man and of the ways in which religion has been often used to provide man with 'the consolation of his fantasies' and so to keep him all the more ready to do nothing about the various chains with which society, its structures and its taken for granted aims surround so many. Unless we are constantly realistic about this we cannot be set free to challenge, as is so urgently necessary, the fundamental error which is contained in this passage. This is the claim that man should be set free 'so that he will revolve about himself as his own true sun'. Here is a fundamental clash in theory and in vision and therefore a constant possibility of a clash also in practice. We believe that for man to 'revolve about himself' is to set him on the way, the way which has been too often and too constantly practised by Christians as well as others, of diminution and dehumanization. Only God as the centre is sufficient for the infinite possibilities of being human. However we cannot make our vital protest on this fundamental point unless we are constantly sensitive to the historical conditions which give accuracy to so much of what Marx says in his diagnosis of religion and so much plausibility to the whole of it. This realism is well indicated in a 'Statement by Sixteen Bishops of the Third World' issued in 1967 and referred to by Herbert McCabe and others in a letter to *The Times* of 27 February 1974. This statement says in part:

[1] Karl Marx, 'Contribution to the Critique of Hegel's Philosophy of Right', quoted from *Early Writings*, ed. and trs. T. B. Bottomore, Watts 1963, pp. 43 f. (slightly altered).

The Church has for a century tolerated capitalism. . . . She cannot but rejoice to see another social system appearing that is less far from her teaching. . . . Far from sulking about it, let us be sure to embrace it gladly as a form of social life better adapted to our times, more in keeping with the spirit of the gospel. In this way we will stop confusing God and religion with the oppressors of the poor and of the workers, which is what the feudal, capitalist and imperialist systems are.

It is with realism in this direction that we must also be realistic about the breakdown of consensus in our society at the present time. We now have no consensus explicit, implicit or capable of being exacted, about the rights and the duties which are involved in our society. There is no consensus either about what it is to be members of society or indeed about what is involved in the very understanding of society as such. We do unquestionably have a great deal of class conflict and conflicts of other sorts, and the critical question is whether our society is to be understood as on the move or simply as breaking down. We therefore have to seek to clear our minds as to where we think society could be moving to and with what resources it can so move. As I have argued in the earlier chapters of this book, we do well to see our uncertainties and disturbances as pointing us to judgment upon the present shape and assumption of our societies. We need therefore to face our present political and social turbulence with some realistic theory and vision which points to the sources of direction, judgment and hope available to us in our struggles to be human. If we believe, as I have argued in chapter 6 that we do, that Christian theory, vision and discipleship is an authentic attempt to live into and to live out of the fundamental realities and energies of the universe, then we must struggle to bring to bear on our present turbulence and uncertainty the understanding which is enshrined in such symbols as those of solidarity in sin, image of God and kingdom of God to which I have referred. To deal with our humanity under threat, in turbulence and in caricature we need, what our Christianity offers us, a theory and a vision of the true image of being and becoming human. That is to say we need a true vision and theory of what men and women can be because of what they are, what is offered to them, and of what they are capable of becoming.

So, if men and women are created in the image of God, with the capacity to develop into that image, which is to be fulfilled in the kingdom, through all that is involved in our living now in solidarity in sin – what then? For, as I have already urged, Christian 'theory' involves 'a sustained pursuit of Christian discipleship in all things'. It is concerned with truth which is being lived into and lived out of and thus established as no mere theory or fantasy. 'What then?' has, therefore, to be worked out as an interacting development of radical spirituality and radical politics. This combination of spirituality and politics, both of which must go to the very roots of things, is, I believe, required by our Christian theory of man.

Spirituality is required, first, because the fulfilment of the potentialities of being human lies in God. Human beings, as I have constantly argued, are in themselves and as themselves claims for the possibilities of love. It is this love which God is, infinite relationship and love which is also universal relationship and love which is at work at all times and in all places to bring about a state of affairs and enjoyment which is commensurate with love. This is the energy at work beyond all structures, all limits or the whole of history but within the historical struggle with structures and limits. This we might call the infinite dimension of being human which requires the practice of spirituality.

Secondly, we are surely clear that men and women are immediately human as well as potentially human, partially human or distortedly human. There is a human quality of depth which corresponds to and responds to the divine quality of depth. Thus there is love now, enjoyment now, being now, awareness now. It is not simply that men and women will be worthwhile, they are worthwhile. Hence we need something in the practice of our discipleship and in the way we struggle to be and become human which is responsive and sensitive now to life, living, energy, being and becoming. We need to be able to be aware that values and being are now present, however contradicted by so much of what goes on and what is done. We may say that this is the vertical dimension which requires us to practise spirituality in being and becoming human.

Further again, obstacles to being human have to be overcome. The most acute of these obstacles is the 'pathology of our identities', i.e., the ways in which these very sources and expressions of identities become the very things which cut us off from our fellow human beings and cause us to ignore, distort and exploit them. This I have referred to at various points from the discussion of 'tribalism' in the first chapter onwards. To overcome this we need the resources of the love of God as they are displayed in the pattern of the incarnation, dying and rising of Jesus. That is to say we need the resources of an identifying, absorbing and overcoming love. We cannot, for example, expect to battle our way into the kingdom of man or of God by means of conflict, destruction and hate and then expect love to emerge. 'I will hate up to and through the revolution. And after the revolution I will abandon hate and then love.'

This reflects a psychologically and practically impossible view of the relational and dynamic aspects of what is involved in being and becoming human. We need, therefore, a spirituality which is concerned to respond to and learn to live from a suffering love which is Transcendence in the midst after the pattern of Jesus Christ, incarnate, crucified and risen.

This, moreover, is the only way of transcending our pathologically expressed and enjoyed identities in the direction of human identities which are truly both fulfilling and fulfilled. For to reach human identities which are capable of contributing to the fulfilment of all human identities and of benefiting from the identities so fulfilled it is clearly necessary that we die to our present identities, i.e., our identities as we at present express them, cherish them and defend them. (It was not merely a manner of speaking to write in the first chapter [p. 12]: 'Nothing less than death and resurrection are involved.')

If, for example, we are all to become fully human through the fulfilled humanness of us all then clearly, my identity as a white bourgeois English Christian must, in *that* form, die. For that form includes much that has denied and still does deny full humanness to some other humans. Moreover that is the only form of identity I at present have. Therefore to achieve my potential identity as a human being I must die to the identity I now have. But, who, with such an identity, is sufficient for these things? Nothing but spirituality, i.e., an openness to the powers and possibilities of the Spirit who is the God who was embodied in the crucified and risen Jesus, can enable this.

Conversely this is precisely what the activity of Jesus Christ is about. Consider, for instance, 'For whosoever would save his life shall lose it: and whosoever shall lose his life for my sake and the gospel shall save it' (Mark 8.35) or 'Except a grain of wheat fall into the earth and die, it abideth by itself alone, but if it die it beareth much fruit' (John 12.24). The energy of the divine love is available to enable human beings to find a way through the obstacles they produce for themselves into relationships which fulfil our identities by transcending these identities.

We may perhaps call this the *suffering* and *overcoming* dimension to go with the *infinite* and *vertical* dimensions involved in human being and becoming and which require the practice of spirituality.

But this very discussion of the need to transcend identities, to die to present identities and to love through to beyond them leads us straight into the historical necessity of the practice of politics.

First, we can no more be pre-Marxist than we can be pre-Freudian – whatever we may hold about the whole theory, metaphysic, mythology and life of either Marx or Freud. We are now alerted as never before to the interconnection and interaction between being human, identity, group, class and tribe. Out of our enlarged understanding of what is involved in being human arises our increased sensitivity to the issues of ideology and of conflict. As to ideology, we know that our very knowing is much more conditioned than we used to think. The way we think about reality and all that surround us is a conditioned set of ideas connected with the group, class, tribe or whatever it may be to which we belong. Similarly with regard to conflict we are now much clearer about the conflicts of interest which exist inevitably in the shape and forms of society as we now have it. The existence therefore of the realities of ideology and of conflict are established beyond doubt whatever disagreement there is or may be about the scope and implications of this existence. Love therefore cannot neglect, ignore or fail to respond to the present causes and expressions of man's inhumanity to man as they are to be found in groups, classes, tribes and the conflicts between them. Such unreality on the part of love would turn love into a fantasy and a romance when, for Christians, love is the very incarnated struggle for, and suffering of, the fulfilment of the whole universe. Indeed, a main theme in the mythology of the Bible is the conflict of love. The story which the Bible is telling, in one of its aspects, is the story of the struggle of God against the powers of evil, against all that contradicts the possibilities which God has created man for and which can be discovered and created from history. Thus we have much talk about the principalities and powers, and this needs to be developed. The metaphor of spiritual warfare and of equipment for this warfare is frequently to be found. Jesus himself is seen as in conflict with the powers which seek to distort and destroy man and his cross is seen as the occasion when he triumphs openly over them. In fact, there is a very main source of gospel life here. That is to say, in this story presentation about the realities with which we are involved, of which we are part and on which we are able to draw, we are shown that we are offered no romantic optimism about progress nor any unrealistic and sentimental approach to the struggles of history and to the struggles of being human. On the other hand there is no pessimistic succumbing to the repeated tragedies and frustrations of the history of man. Rather it is urged that this is the very area of the battle by love for love. The reason that this is a main source of gospel for us is that on reflection it is evident that unless love is involved in our conflicts then it is no love for us. Indeed, it could scarcely be love at all in the sense in which we have been glimpsing it during the exploration on which we have been engaged. A love which is defined by the understanding of a humanness which can be fully human only when all are human and which also understands our full humanness to be of the measure of divinity clearly cannot and must not give up fighting. For everything which is contrary to this everlasting infinite and universal love must be overcome. Moreover we must be able to experience the effects of this love, at least in promise, in the struggles in which we are engeged. Therefore, love (that is to say, Christian love, the love which both proceeds from God, Father, Son and Holy Ghost and the love which is seeking through human beings to be a response to that love) cannot avoid being political, although it is, of course more than that. But to be less is to withdraw from the incarnation and the very promise and purpose of the love which we have.

Secondly, to be a person involves relationship and relationships involve communities. Communities, as we have seen, involve politics. Moreover to be made in the image of God involves response, response involves responsibility and responsibility involves freedom and participation. Men are not made to be dominated but to be freely interdependent. To this end they must struggle towards an *in*dependence which makes them free and responsible givers and receivers of mutual dependence. There are many false, naive and destructive views of freedom around (not least because of the distortions of dominance and the complications of the errors of self-seeking wickedness). But the struggle for freedom is of the essence of being and becoming human. So politics, which are about actual power and actual participation, are inevitable.

Thirdly, the distinctively biblical understanding of men in the world makes it clear that history is where we now have our arena of encounter with God, our place of judgment by God and our opportunities of collaborating with God. Politics, concern for the shape, control and effects of our cities, societies and structures, are therefore a necessary part of meeting God, receiving judgment and responding to him in the building up of human being to fulfilment.

Fourthly, as I tried to show as sharply as possible in the first half of this exploration, it is politics, political stances, choices and privileges which do as much as anything to condemn the church, to make the church a contradiction of the gospel by which and for which it exists. Political repentance is therefore a *sine qua non* of the obedience of the church and of her being freed for the gospel. This requires, first, a recognition that one is in any case involved in politics and then a responsible wrestling with what this involvement has so far meant and what it will now require.

Finally, and perhaps this is really simply a summary or a replacement of all the others, political involvement is demanded by the simple and devastating ways in which human faces are marred and human possibilities denied by 'what goes on in society'. Even if any sort of political success were impossible, sheer human solidarity demands that we should try. Men and women do not deserve that this should be done to them. To deny this urgency is to confess that love is nonsense. And this, surely, we cannot do – especially when we know that love is crucified.

So, however hard it may be to discern the implications or to develop appropriate responses it seems clear that the Christian theoria of man demands the practice of both spirituality and politics. The next thing to say of this practice seems to be that the spirituality and the politics must interact. Men and women are not to be reduced to history, spirituality cannot be reduced to politics and politics cannot fulfil love. On the other hand, incarnation demands that history and politics be taken absolutely seriously, as seriously, indeed, as is required by the presence of the Absolute in history. So we are faced with the necessity of resisting the reduction of one to the other while seeking to put into practice their interaction. I think this will be found to involve mutual challenges between the practice of politics and the practice of spirituality, much collaboration and not a few conflicts. For taking history and politics absolutely seriously as the present arena of being and becoming human implies a conflict with the practice of politics whenever that practice absolutizes politics and history.

A way of following this up is to consider why and in what sense the Christian theory of man, with its consequent implication of the practice and interaction of spirituality and politics, requires also that both the spirituality and the politics should be radical. Here I can proceed simply in an even more sketchy way than I have been proceeding so far. This is for two main reasons over and above the basic feeling of my incompetence and inadequacy. The first is that the practice both of spirituality and of politics must be specific. We are concerned with the concrete actualities and situations in which people live and through which they either develop hope of and hope in their being human or else are distorted and are driven to despair or apathy. Therefore generalizations in this area cannot be of much use. The actual explorations and responses of spirituality and the actual doing of concrete politics can scarcely be described in advance. Secondly the whole area is so controversial and so full of limited and limiting perspectives that dogmatism in advance of experiment is wholly inappropriate. One can only point to what one so far very imperfectly sees and invite to a common exploration and correction. Therefore, with great hesitation, I would make the following points concerning the radicality of both spirituality and politics.

Radical spirituality and radical politics in the sense which is required by the Christian theory of man are bound to be far more critical of what we do and seek by way of either spirituality or politics than we can at the moment see. That is to say 'radical' does and must mean seeking to get to the roots of any current practices or proposals. This is because the spirituality and the politics appropriate to man's true being and destiny have to take us further than we have so far dreamt of or thought feasible. For the aim and direction of such a spirituality and such a politics is to move into God's final future. This is neither defined by nor adequately represented by any set of spiritual responses or any set of political structures we shall achieve here. Both '*semper reformanda*' and 'perpetual revolution' have to be taken seriously. 'Radical' therefore means and must mean 'challenging to the roots' and 'requiring continual uprooting'. It cannot be simply and superficially interpreted as referring to some set of political proposals.

This radicality which involves learning to receive strength and direction for continual uprooting is both a possibility and a necessity because it is concerned with truth. And the truth with which it is concerned is the being and energy of love – which ultimately is the source and the establishment of all reality. The motivation of radical spirituality is to get a clearer insight into and develop a deeper response to the reality of the love of God as reflected in and distorted by other human beings, oneself and the world in which we all live. It is not to fit into a pattern already understood and received. The motivation of radical politics is not to fit men and structures into a pattern already ideologically understood but to break out of structures ideologically determined and to set free human beings who are structurally and ideologically confined. The aim is that more people should get more space to be human and in this shall be able to perceive and create signs and foretastes of that full development of human reality which lies, as we Christians would put it, in the kingdom. This means, I believe, that the basic concern of radical politics is how to enable people to be aware that they count, not how to solve their problems for them.

Radical spirituality and radical politics involves the pattern of the Transcendence in the midst embodied and lived out by Jesus – that is the pattern of identification, cross and resurrection. The mode of the practice of spirituality and of politics is thus not that exposed in seeking after my/our spiritual development or my/our achievement of political leadership and success. It is rather the mode of compassion – of seeking a suffering with the suffering love of God and the suffering humanity who are to be served. This is almost unbelievably difficult. But for the sake of keeping ways open towards the development of a true humanness it is absolutely essential that this attempt be made. We must look to God to lead us into this grace. As I have already pointed out in chapter 6 (see p. 77), it is a terrible thing when people prefer their theory, whether political or theological, to a concern for the realities of being and becoming human as it is reflected in the faces of actual men and women. Hence a sensitivity which may at any moment move into suffering is an essential part of a radical spirituality and a radical politics which goes deep enough into the roots of what it is and what it may be to be human. The grace which we must look for here will include the gift of tears, that is to say the spiritual energy and freedom to weep tears of joy with those who rejoice and tears of sorrow with those who suffer. This enables some justice to be done to human immediacy. The gift, if given and received, will represent a passion of compassion which will replace the passion of hate without any loss of urgency and with a great release of healing and reconciliation.

Radical spirituality and radical politics will also refuse all false and premature simplifications. This is because of the connection with truth and with faith. Our commitment is to live more and more deeply into what there truly is, so that we may live out of the reality encountered. Thus spirituality must live with loneliness, loss, uncertainty – and face the possibility and reality of having lost a way and of seeing as yet no way. Not knowing and facing not knowing is an essential part of facing human reality and receiving growth in it. Likewise radical politics must avoid falling for simplifications such as the determining of policy by the projection of false or partial scapegoats. Radical politics must also recognize the limits of human possibilities and situations and not disturb and distress with false hopes. Misery can be doubled by inflating hopes and so inflating the sense of deprivation and dissatisfaction. In fact radical politics and radical spirituality must be truly human politics and spirituality and not the practices of fantastic supermen, misplaced demigods or disappointed animals. Hence an attempt must be made to develop a pattern of practice which takes on the shape of the God-man who suffered and died as a truly human being but rose again. No other pattern either faces reality to its depth or moves reality towards its true glory, a glory which is at the same time both human and divine.

Can anything more be said about what all this might mean in practice? Here we must return to and go on from the discussion in chapter 4 about 'judgment from the poor and the excluded'. We must take up again the positive side of our understanding of the insights and challenges of Marxism. We have also to remember, as I said earlier in this chapter, that 'the actual explorations and responses of spirituality and actual doing of concrete politics can scarcely be described in advance'. None the less it does seem at least to be clear that as Christians we must abandon conservatism and face towards revolution. In the light of the whole discussion so far I hope that it is sufficiently clear that a statement of this nature does not imply that 'Conservatives' are thereby designated as those who have no Christian commitment, still less as those who can expect no part in the kingdom of God. The rejection of the absolutizing of both history and politics implies also the rejection of the notion that our eternal destiny or salvation is fully and finally determined by the parts we play in history and politics. However, the assertion that we are all ultimately and finally dependent on God for our human fulfilment and salvation does not imply that we are thereby absolved from the responsibility of understanding as clearly as possible what God now requires of us and of attempting to meet that requirement. In chapter 4 I pointed out how 'the city reflects the humanly destructive trends at work among us' (p. 49). The issue which is raised by perceiving these 'humanly destructive trends' is a pressing and fundamental question about the nature and possibilities of human life and human community.

How are we to read the signs of the times and in what context shall we understand such essentially relative terms as 'underprivileged', 'dispossessed', 'marginal'? (cf. the discussion in chapter 4). For example, does one start from the position that 'the poor are always with us', that all systems function more or less well or badly but with some degree of inefficiency, that there always will be marginals and that therefore society must do its best to extend charity and help to these marginals, to channel a portion of its resources into alleviating the conditions and causes of marginalization, and to be constantly open to the possibility of new reforms to deal with these problems? The focus of interest remains, however, the advance of 'society as a whole' and the marginals remain marginals. That is to say, the problem of the poor is one of the problems of society, a problem which must never be forgotten but just one of the problems nevertheless.

Or does one hold with the Marxist that the urban proletariat are the decisive key to both the sicknesses of society and the way forward to a more human society? And how should one respond to the convergence, resonance and overlap there is between this view and the prophetic tradition in the bible which sees 'the poor' as central to the diagnosis of the sins of society and as the special object of God's concern so that issues of social justice are essentially connected both with the judgment of God and with the kingdom of God?

As I have already argued, it seems clear that a Christian is obliged to find his or her position somewhere in the area of the second option rather than the first. The poor and the marginals are not primarily objects of charity and compassion but rather subjects and agents of the judgment of God and pointers to the ways of the kingdom. God is the Disturber of all those conditions and sins of men, both as individuals and as societies, which stand in the way of development towards a fully human society.

Our cities draw attention to the extent to which our present ways of conducting our affairs are dehumanizing. Just as the cities are breaking down or have, for many, already broken down as ways of promoting human community and human living, so they force attention to the ways in which the basic assumptions and strategies of our societies have something essentially dehumanizing in them. So we are brought to the point where we have to recognize that it is the system which must be under attack for the sake of humanity.

The crux, however, lies in how we understand 'for the sake of humanity', and it is here, I believe, that the convergence between necessarily revolutionary attacks on the system and the understanding of God as the Disturber for the sake of human community becomes most clear. God's concern for mankind is clearly universal; he has no favourites but loves all equally and infinitely. Where he chooses he chooses for the sake of his universal saving purposes. (It is one more devastating piece of evidence about human sin that this divine choice is again and again understood as human privilege. The locus classicus here is, of course, the epistle to the Romans.) The kingdom of God is where all men are to be fulfilled by sharing in the community of the love of God. The powers of the kingdom of God are those which are at work to deal with disease, sin and death and set men free for 'life more abundant'. The notion that this abundant life is nothing but an individual possession in a wholly future heaven is, we can now see, a manifest distortion of the whole thrust of the biblical picture of God at work in history for human salvation and wholeness. It has, moreover, become an essentially political and ideological distortion whereby ultimate privilege in heaven for the chosen few is linked to maintenance of privilege on earth.

God has never allowed such distortions to be permanent. He bestows one privilege and one privilege only: that of receiving the infinite resources both of his judgment and of his love so that men and women may be partakers in, and servants of, the ever-expanding work of his kingdom. Neither Israel nor Judah, Jewish people nor Christian church, imperial Christendom nor dominating Christian civilization are allowed to remain in positions of privilege and power when they arrogate to themselves exclusive rights and become more concerned with the preservation of a status quo reflecting the past than with the struggle for a future which is more generally shared.

Thus the pressure of God and his kingdom upon us at the present time is particularly to be seen in the rapid spread of the discovery that *everybody* is human and even more particularly in the rapid growth of the *awareness* of everybody that they too are human. This is the essential theological, political and practical point and the reason why social justice is now such a central and such a totally disturbing issue on which neutrality is impossible for a Christian. There are two reasons for being concerned to fight against the status quo and 'the system' as it operates in most of the countries of the world and, in an interlocking way, throughout the world. The first is operative for all the underprivileged and oppressed. 'They' oppress 'us', therefore 'we' must get on top of, or at least equal with, them. If there is a belief in justice and the possibility of justice, then this is a cry for justice. If it is assumed that the world is simply a place of random struggle, then this is a struggle of the have-nots to become the haves.

Which leads us to the second reason for being against 'the system'. This is the understanding that the system is unjust and justice must be fought for. But what *is* justice? Supposing the proposition 'there is no justice in the world for the majority of men, women and children living in the world' is simply a statement about the nature of the world? Then we are faced with a mere power struggle between the haves and the have-nots. This, however, is clearly unacceptable and unbelievable for Christians. A righteous God is at work in the world, for the world and beyond the world. Consequently the concern for justice is possible, necessary and a joyful challenge.

But it is to be noted that the cry for justice is most important when it emerges at what might almost be called the 'amoral' level, that is, when 'we' (who are oppressed, underprivileged, marginalized) insist that we have as much right to the good things of the world as 'they'. For the elementary determination to be or to get 'as good as them' indicates the dawning awareness that 'we' are as human *in every way* as 'they' are. Exploitation, privilege, dominance are no longer taken for granted because everyone is realizing that he or she is as equally human as anyone else. Thus the widespread and spreading refusal of the underprivileged, the dispossessed and the marginals to accept their lot is a widespread recognition of the *universal* potential of what is to be human.

Now this universal potential of being human is precisely what God has demonstrated by becoming man. This is why the so-called revolutionary ferments of our present world have to be recognized as related to and relatable to the kingdom of God. (There is no straightforward total equivalence or romantic equation in every detail, because sin is not confined to the oppressors and the poor are not made holy by their determined and exacted poverty.) Thus the threats to the present system which are so sharply presented in our cities must be seen by Christians as real threats both to power as it is at present exercised and to conscience as it is at present informed. The present privileged *are* being attacked and they (we) *ought* to be attacked. There is a demand to repent in practical, structural and political ways for all those things in the present systems which promote and often accelerate such manifest and inhuman injustice. We cannot expect just to reform our cities. We have to change our ways of life 'for the sake of being human', that is, to take account of the fact that every man, woman and child is equally destined to be a full human being and that God is at work in and through history to this end.

I do not think that this understanding enables us to know what 'social justice' would mean in any fulfilled sense (the vision of the kingdom of heaven remains inevitably unclear) nor does it provide us with any simple blueprints or prescriptions for local, national or international political action. It does however suggest certain perspectives for us. Above all it suggests that we Christians have to understand that the ultimate strategy of the kingdom of God is *revolutionary* and that this is a sober truth which must be reckoned with, despite all the rhetoric and falsity which is bound up with this over-used term. This is to recognize the need and right of the majority of men and women to 'revolutionize' the systems which leave them, or treat them, as less than human, as not entitled to the same rights, possibilities and hopes as other human beings. Such a transformation of both power and practice is involved here that no word weaker than 'revolutionize' will do. For the forces and trends reflected so clearly in our cities make it clear that it is not within the intentions, let alone the capacities, of the principles and practices of our present economic and political lives to promote anything like a just share in the possibilities of being human. Nothing less than a revolution must come about.

But it is not at all clear that men are willing and able to either produce or allow required revolutions any more than they are willing to repent in the ways required to permit the growth of wider and more loving styles of life. Further, revolutions have no built-in guarantee of continuing success in furthering justice and humanity. We are thus faced not only with the tussle between 'reform' and 'revolution' but also with the ever-present possibility of 'apocalypse'. Society as a whole or particular parts within it may come to breakdown. Conflicts may become uncontrollable. None the less, I cannot escape the conclusion that the revolutionary pressures of the poor against the privileged are, in the main, the material of, or at least the material for, the furtherance of the kingdom of God. This kingdom of God will advance, not by overruling history but by continuing to work in history.

We cannot, therefore, expect anything but an increase in revolutionary situations and disturbances. Christians should neither expect nor wish to be able to contain these disturbances by a strategy either of conservatism or reform. Radical repentance, radical change and radical redistribution of power and privilege are overwhelmingly required by the realities of the kingdom of God and the possibilities of being human. *Tactics* of conservatism or reform may, of course, be possible, necessary and human political options in given situations. But I believe that as Christians we have to face the reality that any overall policy of conservatism or reform as a lasting way of life is impossible and undesirable. The demand of both God and man are much more severe and much more creative than that.

It seems, however, that there is very little chance of enough willing revolutionary change fast enough over a wide enough range. Hence the apocalyptic element in our situation. Explosions or implosions of various local, national (and therefore, potentially of international) situations are bound to occur. How apocalyptic these outbursts or collapses will become no one can know. It is clear, however, that if they are chiefly treated as terrifying examples of violence to be suppressed, rather than as signs of judgment upon a too slow and too insensitive response to the pressures of social injustice, then the apocalyptic element in the situation will grow. This is where the overall understanding of our Christian faith and our beliefs about the kingdom of God are, or should be, so important. Do we believe that the increasing fierceness of the fight for social justice by so many groups, races and classes who hitherto have had little influence in the development of history is to be understood as a negative 'growth in violence and instability' or as positive signs to be related to the kingdom of God?

Ambiguity is inescapable. But despair, indifference or consistent opposition can only guarantee apocalypse. Something much more positive and hopeful is surely offered to us with the help of the biblical portrayal of the activities of God and with the proclamation of the gospel of the resurrection of Jesus. More and more men and women are claiming the right to be human. How this right can be achieved and how exercised in relation to all the perplexities, complexities and distortions of actual human living is a matter of great uncertainty. But the possibilities and the resources exist in the purposes and energies of God. Therefore, we have to find ways and means of welcoming and sharing the revolutionary developments that are required, facing apocalyptic threats and, it may be, enduring apocalyptic situations in hope and of playing our part in such temporary or partial reforms as immediate situations and opportunities shall require.

We have, in fact, to learn to live once more as strangers and pilgrims on earth with no 'abiding city' (no indissoluble or essential status quo) because we are all travelling towards the city of God which will fulfil and surpass the cities and communities of men.

As our present point of entry into the pilgrimage, and into the learning of what is involved in seeking to relate the kingdom of God to the struggles of men for a social justice which cannot but be revolutionary, we are faced with the challenge of what I will call our 'local marginals'. That is to say that we are called to discern the signs of the kingdom by struggling to find ways of working with some of those whom our own community or state or nation now refuses to treat as equally human with the privileged and established. We are *not* called to offer charity to the aged, or to some marginalized ethnic group or to some area of poverty and delinquency. We are called to risk finding ways of involvement with 'the marginals' in a common search for a wider human identity. It is not a question of our helping them but of finding common ways of action which will liberate and change the identity of us all. For what is at issue is the enlargement of humanity. And this comes about by mutual sharing and equal opportunities to contribute and to count. Essentially it is not some abstract 'justice' which men require but the opportunity to be themselves. Hence 'marginals' are not to be 'helped'. They have to become full partners in a common enterprise.

In a proper Christian understanding I believe that revolution and repentance should and would go very closely together. Structurally there is a battle to break out of dehumanizing institutions and move towards wider sharing of power and of opportunity. Personally there is a battle to learn what it is to be a servant and a neighbour. Our present Christian opportunity is to learn how these two battles go together in the struggle for social justice and the increasing freeing of men and women to be human in their own ways in positive relation to the ways and needs of others.

9

Concerning violence and more about contradiction

It has been necessary during the course of this exploration to go to and fro between the complexities and perplexities of our human problems and the hopes and visions with which we face them or which we may discern in the midst of them. This necessity is both human and, from a Christian point of view, theological. The necessity is human because we are involved in all these complexities and perplexities. All these pressures, threats, contradictions and possibilities press in upon us and affect us both from within and from without. It is certain that all this is part of the reality which both affects and constitutes us. Is this all the reality there is or is there more? So we are obliged to struggle, explore and enquire between perplexities and hope, between contradictions and visions. For a Christian this necessity is also theological. Jesus Christ is believed to embody the commitment of God to the world and the energy of God for the fulfilment of the world. Thus Christian discipleship, the attempt to respond to God through Jesus Christ in and in collaboration with the Spirit of God, requires a full involvement in the offers, struggles and sufferings of being and becoming human. This is so because Jesus Christ expresses and embodies the reality and offer of God to us through involvement in the struggles and sufferings of being human. I wish to close the exploration and argument of this book by returning to the Vision and by seeking to give some description of what I believe to be the offer of the kingdom of God made through Jesus Christ to all men and women. But first I feel obliged to take one more look at the truly agonizing perplexities with which we must live before I sketch a final glimpse of the hope which lies both in these perplexities and beyond them. This necessity arises because, for me, Jesus Christ points decisively to ultimate reality. Hence faith in God through him and the practice of Christian discipleship absolutely demand that we face as fully as we can the actualities and implications of immediate realities.

The Christian gospel of the love of God is a total claim and vision about reality and it is pinned to our history decisively and definitely by the life and death of Jesus. This is why we can dare to claim, and are free to claim, that love *is* the ultimate and fulfilling reality of all things. Because Jesus Christ suffered and died, we know that love bears the contradiction of love. Therefore love will not be and cannot be finally contradicted. Love is neither romantic nor unrealistic. It is involved in conflict and pays the price necessary to establish its purposes in and through such a world as ours is. So the crucified Jesus Christ is of universal significance not because he is risen but because he is one with Father and with Holy Spirit, one in and as the energy and power of love. It is his resurrection which proclaims this to us and releases the knowledge of the universal scope and suffering of love into the world. The Trinity, which is the symbol of the unity of the life of Jesus with the whole life and energy of God, is thus the symbol of our hope in and for the universal society of love. (It is of this that I try to write a little more in the next and final chapter.)

But we have this life, and live by and for this hope, precisely because love lives in and through the conflicts and the contradictions of human and historical living. Hence it was perfectly proper and, as I believe, necessary in our particular historical circumstances to examine what we now know about the obstacles to being human in our present human societies and to examine what is alleged about these obstacles. This was why I tried in chapters 3–5 to consider the diagnoses and challenges of Marxism. I believe that Marxism convicts us of much structural, ideological and class sin, and that this conviction of sin is fully supported by what the Bible presents to us about the poor and the excluded as crucial indications of the judgment of God upon the sins of society. However, any Christian understanding and vision of men obliges us to deny the Marxist doctrine of man and to insist that man is neither confined to history nor determined by ideological, structural and class factors. Human sin goes deeper and human possibilities extend further – in fact to the depths and infinities indicated by man as created in the image of God and destined for the kingdom of God.

Yet – again – our part in the human struggle for the emergence, expression and achievement of love is, for us, an historical part. Hence, our Christian discipleship which is our search for truly human being and becoming is a matter both of radical spirituality and of radical politics. We look for and depend upon a Transcendent future and a Transcendent Power but now we are experiencing and responding to Transcendence in the midst – and this is in the midst of our human struggles which are, inevitably, political struggles.

Therefore, in my last chapter I tried to point to some of the elements which are involved in the interpenetration and interaction between a radical spirituality and a radical politics, in pursuance of my fundamental conviction that love does not turn away from history although love is not confined to history. My arguments led me to say: 'I cannot escape the conclusion that the revolutionary pressures of the poor against the privileged are, in the main, the material of, or at least the material for, the furtherance of the kingdom of God. This kingdom of God will advance, not by overruling history but by continuing to work in history' (ch. 8, p. 119). If this is at all a correct conclusion then it is wholly unrealistic to proceed to any description, however slight and inadequate, of a final vision and hope without making some attempt to face the question and the reality of violence. We have had to refer a good many times to the inevitability of conflict. Conflict without violence is rarely possible, or at least, violence is always a possibility and often occurs. How then, are we to face these realities of conflict and violence? Something, it seems, must be said on this as an attempt to reflect the vision of men and women in the image of God and destined for the kingdom of God into the actual struggles which we face and of which we have to be a part. As Jesus is seen and known as standing for the involvement of God in our struggles, any understanding or vision which is held to obtain its truth and validity 'through Jesus Christ' must likewise undergo such an involvement. Hence the internal logic and dynamic of my exploration forces me to sketch out what I have so far perceived of the implications of this involvement. After I have done this, I will comment further on what is implied by the extremely inadequate and unsatisfying nature of these perceptions.

First, then, there is the connection of violence in society with judgment on society. Violence related to political aims, including much that is described as 'terrorism', and which is promoted by persons and groups claiming 'freedom', is largely to be understood as the pathological effects of the violence which various societies do perpetrate in various forms against legitimate and, often, basic human aspirations. The violent are representatives of groups who have had great violence done to their aspirations and hopes for being as human as everyone else. Christians have to be alert to receive and to perceive the disturbances which God directs against those features of society which work against the full value of human beings. It is clearly, therefore, very important to evaluate that element of violence directed against society or to further political aims which is symptom rather than cause. The primary and continuing response to such violence must be to discern the wider causes and the deeper oppressions of which it is symptomatic. Men are denied 'the kingdom' and have become increasingly aware of it – and aware also that their fellow men are instruments of this denial. Further, this primary response which is required of us must include genuinely positive steps to remove or mitigate these structural and political causes of man's denial of humanity to man. A primary response to this type of conflict and violence which insists solely on the maintenance of law and order is to deny judgment and to provoke further judgment. Violence must be understood within the context of the human revolution and of the search of men and women for an equal human dignity.

But, secondly, humanly speaking it must be maintained that for human beings face-to-face relationships are primary or basic rather than structural ones. Hence the actual committing of violent acts – bombs, killings, beatings up (whether by 'freedom forces' or by 'the forces of law and order') – is a form of violence for which there is more direct personal responsibility than for the incidental effects of what is sometimes referred to as 'structural violence' (for instance, the fact that the structure of society 'does violence to me' by keeping me poor). Further, violence is also a particularly fruitful field for the expression of human wickedness and always pathological as such. Therefore the personal perpetrators of organized and specific violence directed consciously against particular persons can never be regarded as heroes, no matter what side they are on, and they must take responsibility for their part in wickedness. Whatever tactics of conflict, even of hate, seem inevitable in some particular situations, the basic question must always remain 'How can *you* humanize by inhuman action?' And this 'How can *you*?' is addressed to the 'you' who act as an acting self or acting selves and not as an abstract group. The personal question cannot be depersonalized away into statements about 'the poor', 'the oppressed', 'the underprivileged'. When we commit violence, we are not doing it primarily 'on behalf of', we are *doing it*, perpetrating violence against other human beings.

The term 'structural violence' is a metaphor, although it refers to a reality. Personal violence is an act, and an act which can never be condoned even if it has to be committed, and which is the human personal responsibility of those who commit it. Conversely, however, the forces of 'law and order' and the preservers of the status quo must not use this argument to justify themselves. To all the message is: 'Except you repent you will all likewise perish.'

Thirdly, therefore, it is clear that organized personal violence is, at the very 'best', a weapon of the very last resort which can be chosen only under extremes of injustice and immobility in response. There are, I would hold, no situations in the British Isles or in Ireland which can be rightly judged to amount to such extremes, although – once again – it is absolutely essential to maintain that there is great injustice and much unforgivable immobility in response, so that responsibility for what violence there is has to be shared more widely than simply among those who commit the violence.

Fourthly, I am inclined to believe that Christians should be the last to initiate violence – or perhaps, should never initiate violence. It is, I think, quite clearly impossible to reconcile the actual practice of Jesus Christ with the practice of violence – whatever people may say. He demonstrated and exercised the power of the Son who was totally dependent on the Father and so totally open to all that men did to him. Therefore he demonstrated the power of powerlessness which is the all-absorbing power of absolute love. He is uncompromising Transcendence in the midst who judges us all.

However, I do not believe that our ethical dilemmas can be settled by a simple appeal to the imitation of Jesus. We neither have his historical mission nor share his precise personal situation. It may, therefore, be that to us the way of the power of powerlessness is not open. But we must not justify any other way by twisting what Jesus was and did and the way he went. We can only accept the sinful necessity, when and if it arises, of choosing one side of violence rather than another. Hence, as I see it, the need for Christians to be the last to initiate or never to initiate violence. (On the matter of Jesus and the power of powerlessness something more needs to be said. See shortly below.)

The Christian hesitation concerning violence is, I think, reinforced by the Christian understanding that there are sources and resources of reconciliation which give grounds for hope beyond any immediate human hope. Above all, Christians do not expect the ultimate fulfilment of human being and becoming through political action. All such action is therefore always provisional and never absolute. It is not possible, therefore, to say finally: *This* is the only way. Such a judgment is always provisional and liable to revision and repentance after it has been made and acted upon. So – as far as I can see – the compulsion to violence can never be as absolute for a Christian as for others more historically confined. This would, therefore, reinforce practical Christian hesitancy which may well have to be expressed and acted upon despite taunts (which may have other social justifications) about unreadiness for commitment. But the question always remains, 'Commitment to what or for whom ?'

Nevertheless, fifthly, it seems to me inescapable that Christians may find themselves obliged to share in policies which involve violent action where responsible reflection endorses the judgment of others that an extreme situation of oppression and injustice is present and is, at present, apparently immovable. The most likely grounds for leading Christians to this type of action will be the realization that to remain uncommitted at a certain historical juncture is equivalent to commitment to those oppressors who are clearly, blatantly and extremely oppressive.

It is here that we return to a point which I touched on earlier when I drew attention to the fact that the responsibility for decisions of such a type must lie with the Christians in a particular region or country. I would like to reinforce this by arguing that on the one hand Christians must respect the decisions taken by their fellows in differing circumstances. On the other there must be mutual accountability between Christians of varying situations who take different decisions about why they hold their decisions to be required of them as *Christians* in *this* situation.

I further believe that the provisionality of all political decisions and the Transcendence of the ultimate future which is offered to human beings should prevent one set of Christians from 'excommunicating' another set on the grounds of their political judgments and action. On the one hand, no one can be absolutely sure that their judgment and action is right, still less that it is righteous. On the other hand, persons are not cut off from the love of God because they are in the wrong. This, I think, must apply as much to crucial matters to do with freedom and oppression as to any other crucial area of human intercourse and action.

It may be thought that the above five points on reflecting about violence have made the matter too complicated already. Reference, however, must be made to the discussion about radical spirituality and radical politics in which it was pointed out that getting to the roots of things requires a concern for truth and reality in all their complexity. I feel it necessary, therefore, to add one more consideration. Thus, sixthly, it is, surely, an illusion to suppose that any society here on earth will ever be able to be maintained without some form of socially licensed violence to protect itself and its members against violence. That is to say, some form of 'police force' will be inevitable.

There seem to be no grounds in anyone's theory of society (Marxist, Christian or other) for holding that a society can be kept in being and operating without some framework that involves some degree of compulsion. Until perfect beings exist in a perfected society, there will be friction between the requirements of any framework and the activities and desires of some, at least, of those living in society. Indeed, the costs of running any society will, seemingly, include various forms of injustice and dissatisfaction to various members and groups of that society. The struggle is to see these for what they are and to work (and it may be fight) for more even sharing and bearing of these costs, in so far as they cannot be removed. The illusion is to suppose that no such costs have to be incurred or paid.

There is, further, the question of wickedness. This may be an unfashionable notion, not least because self-appointed definers and detectors of 'wickedness' have made this a supple weapon for dehumanizing and oppressing others who threaten their powers and privileges. But a decision about the nature of human reality has to be made here. It seems to me clear that being human includes the capacity to be cruel, not because one is driven to it but because one desires and chooses it, and that men and women can and do find the fulfilment of their own humanness in the deliberate destruction of the humanness of others. This contradiction goes so deep and is, in its effects and implications, so terrifying, that it is no wonder that various scientific, psychological, philosophical and ideological attempts are made to explain this contradiction away. Most of them make some contributions to identifying the complexities of human action and sin and so have the capacity to contribute to more compassionate and understanding responses to and in these complexities. None the less, I believe that they all end up in various versions of a lie. They will not face up to how terrible a thing it can be to be human. This is the other side of how glorious a thing it can be to be human. (I refer back to my discussion in chapter 7 of how our view of what is wrong in being human is part of our understanding and hope of what is and can be right with being human.) Thus our vocabulary for describing human and social reality cannot effectively do without some word such as 'wickedness' which refers to a tendency among men and women, individually and in groupings, sometimes to prefer to promote that which is evil and destructive and to enjoy doing this. Thus, any society and its members will require some arrangements for coercive protection against, and putting limitations on, the exercise of such wickedness. This remains true even though diagnoses of 'wickedness' can be wickedly wrong and measures against 'wickedness' can be wickedly misused. We have therefore to attempt to fight against accepting the inevitability of oppressive violence while we at the same time attempt to live with the likely ambiguity and inevitability of protective violence. I do not think that our problem, dilemma and even agony is solved by insisting that a distinction between 'violence' and 'force' is simple, obvious and necessary. 'Violence', it might be held, is socially and individually wrong, while 'force' is often socially necessary and legitimate. Such a distinction too often helps to legitimate violent means used by those in power to put down those with human claims against those powers; it also obscures the complexities and ambiguities of our social and human situations and often fails to take account of the inhuman effects and possibilities of force and violence in all situations where they happen or are held to be necessary.

Thus we have one more indication, in considering the relationship between society and human nature, of the practical impossibility of being absolute about the use or non-use of violence. It further reinforces the ambiguity and tension with which we have to live. For this 'police violence' (as I am calling it) will also have its pathological elements (as a human and a social activity). There will be personal wickedness in the expression both of 'anti-social' violence and in the expression of violence against those who are 'anti-social'. There will also be conflicts about what sort of society is worth protecting and preserving and by what means. And all this will be so whether the balance of 'structural violence' lies with the supporters of the fabric of society or with those who attack it. Hence Christians, while they must refuse to absolutize being either for or against law and order, must accept the responsibility to share in monitoring all the activities of the guardians of society and protectors of the law. Where occasion requires, these activities must be exposed and attacked. Since we know we have no abiding city, we must be very clear that what I will call 'the present city police force' can be no more assumed to be righteous than any other institution whatever.

Further, the possibility must constantly be faced that in extremes 'police' violence can become wholly pathological – not necessarily because of the individual wickedness of 'policemen' (although this may well contribute), but because of the pathology of the structures. Here, however, it is also necessary to return to the understanding of 'solidarity in sin' about which I argued in my fifth chapter. This should help us to face the fact that, in situations of pathological police violence, policemen also are trapped human beings.

(It should be clear that in the immediately preceding paragraphs I am using the word 'police' with deliberate ambiguity and unclarity. Members of forces that are actually designated 'police' are by no means the only personnel of these coercive/protective structures which, in any given society, constitute 'the present city police force'. I employ ambiguity because it seems necessary to provoke a good deal more reflection and sense of reality about these matters than is often displayed. It is quite clear that 'the problem of the police' in the technical sense of police forces and the problems facing actual policemen must be placed in the wider context of society, its aims and actual effects. I believe, also, that both supporters of our form of society and attackers of it unite on many occasions in making the police the scapegoats for and on behalf of society. Supporters of society expect the police to do their dirty work for them and to remain exceptionally righteous while performing this task. Sufferers from society can blame the police for everything that happens to them. Such attitudes and pressures do not do justice to the police as actual human beings and may well also encourage in them increasing brutality and violence as the actual handling of the vicious effects of the polarities of society is left to them. It seems to me particularly important that Christians should not formulate or express attitudes to and opinions about violence and force which show no sensitivity to what it is like to suffer the violences of society or to be left by society to handle the violent effects and counter-effects of the violences.)

One thing seems to be clear through all the complications to which I have been referring. This is that Christians cannot take refuge from the ambiguities, costs, and risks of various situations by withdrawing to some position held to be above the struggle. Christian balance and poise with regard to these struggles does not consist in an indifference, a distaste or an effortless ease which is above the struggles. It consists rather in the maintenance of a suffering tension which is poised for energetic and involved response and then strained towards reflection and repentance. There can be no escape from the necessity to judge and to act and then to receive judgment and renewal. Whether, for the time being, as Christians we seek neutrality or whether we seek involvement we must always look for grace to enter into the cost of our calling. The pattern of Christian response is resurrection through the cross. A cheap neutrality is not Christian and will usually support an oppressive status quo. There may be occasions when there has to be a refusal to take a particular part in a particular struggle. But this will be legitimately and truly Christian only when it is a costly standing-out against a particular resolution of a particular situation on the grounds that greater hopes and greater possibilities must be witnessed to.

With regard to these greater hopes and greater possibilities, it is now necessary to return to the matter of Jesus and the power of powerlessness to which I made reference above (p. 125). I have already said that it is clearly impossible to reconcile the actual practice of Jesus Christ with the practice of violence and that he is uncompromising Transcendence in the midst who judges us all. The extent to which he judges us and the position in which this leaves us needs to be made clearer. To assist in this I now include in this chapter a short document which I wrote originally during a consultation organized by the joint Roman Catholic/World Council of Churches Secretariat on Society, Development and Peace (SODEPAX). The subject of the consultation was Theology and Development and it was held at Cartigny, Switzerland in November 1969.[1] Father Gutierrez contributed a paper, 'Notes on a Theology of Liberation', which, as he says in the introduction to his book, sketched the lines of thought which he works out in his full-length study. His contribution and others, and the very nature of the subject, meant that many searching questions were raised about power, the struggle for power and Christian attitudes to these struggles. In the midst of these discussions I found certain troubling questions crystallizing in my mind. When I tentatively voiced these I was asked to prepare a hastily written note, and so the following emerged under the title of 'The Power of the Powerless'.

> The following note raises some questions, the direct application of which to development and the involvement of the churches in development is probably neither obvious nor generally agreed. None the less, on the assumption that there is any truth in Christianity, these questions have to be borne in mind.
>
> The basic question is: How seriously do we have to take Jesus Christ who is portrayed in the gospels as a real embodiment in historical conditions of the presence and power of the Kingdom of God? (The fact that this is a basic question which the churches have always avoided and which Christians generally disagree about is no reason for avoiding or forgetting the question.)
>
> On the face of it, the presentation of the New Testament is that when God gets down to work on earth in a personal and definitive manner he exhibits his power in powerlessness. The forsaken and crucified man is believed to be the Christ of God. (Literally so and personally so – that was why he came to be worshipped, acknowledged as Lord and, eventually, declared to be 'of one substance with the Father'. The last declaration may be said to be 'Greek metaphysics' and mistaken ontology. But is the insight of faith wrong? What is the significance of Jesus for the Christian?) The New Testament appears to be built on the conviction that Jesus is the way God works.
>
> This appears to suggest that the ultimate power which is capable of

[1] See the report, *In Search of a Theology of Development*, World Council of Churches, Geneva 1970; quotation from pp. 51–3.

bringing in and establishing the Kingdom of God is the love of God (the God who is love), which love exhibits its power as powerlessness.

This is very difficult to believe and even more difficult to live up to or out of (it clearly involves the Cross from the beginning of history to its end). But it is possible to see that it might be the only hope of an eventual establishment of a Kingdom of love in which man might be really fulfilled. Power as we know it (powerful power and not powerless power) always involves counter-action and counter-effects. Oppression forces either despair or revolt. Revolution produces counter-revolution, or else the 'revolutionaries' become counter-revolutionary to hold on to their power. In personal relations only the soft answer turns away wrath (sometimes). Wrath creates new waves of resentment and so on.

If (and it is a big 'if'!) we are ever to get to a state of equilibrium in which all are fulfilled in each other and each can enjoy all (a creative Kingdom of love) then there must be a power at work which will *absorb* powerful power rather than *counter* power with power. If Christians believe that there is such a power, the power of God as embodied in Jesus Christ, how does this affect their attitudes and responses to the 'powerful' sort of power (i.e. power as the world and its institutions, including the churches, know and practise it)?

Presumably Christians will *not* believe that the use of 'powerful' power will ever produce a satisfactory and lastingly human state of affairs. Hence they will regard *all* uses of powerful power as interim and as the lesser of two evils (at the best). They may perhaps further conclude that if ever and wherever this powerful power is used it can at most only break up an intolerable situation. It cannot build a tolerable one. That can only be built by the 'powerless' power, the love that absorbs, suffers and so reconciles. To build any creative human society (and not one which is just a repetition of an old power structure with the components arranged differently) it is *literally* necessary to love your enemy (in the class struggle, the revolution, the schism – or what you will!).

Further, as Christians we presumably have to find ways of practising real repentance about the involvement of the churches as institutions with power structures and the 'powers that be'. It is almost certainly a mistake to want any church which has power in these structures to use it *as* a power and pressure group. This is simply to play the power game. Repentance probably does *not* mean going over from being a 'power' on the side of the government to being a similar sort of 'power' on the side of the poor and oppressed. It probably means finding the creative and costly way of becoming powerless.

In any case, any power which an institution has it will have because it is an institution and not because it is a *Christian* institution, and those who exercise its institutional power must become aware that something more than the exercise of institutional power is required for any involvement or activity to be specifically Christian and capable of real creativity and reconciliation.

It might well be, therefore, that the challenge to any church which really wishes to be a Christian organic activity and not to protect its life as a mere religious institution is to be ready to lose power and face powerfully and hopefully the question of powerlessness.

Once again, we can glimpse practical grounds for this which are not directly related to Jesus' embodiment of God's power in powerlessness. The power of the powerful is both limited and limiting. On the one hand utopian expectations of a liberation which will overthrow the powers that be and produce a state of liberty where there is no restrictive power and all men are free to enjoy a full life to the full are clearly only dreams. They may be inspiring, encouraging and creative dreams but there remains the need to give life, meaning and hope to those who, for *their* lives, will remain part of the powerless and the restricted. On the other hand the power of the powerful is also strictly limited. No matter who is 'in power' and what their resources are, what can be done, consciously or unconsciously, does not amount to anything like a total control of any situation or future. Hence men simply have to live with powerlessness as well as with power.

It may be that it is somehow in this connection that we have to relate the biblical significance of 'the poor' to problems of power and powerlessness. There is at least a tendency in the Bible to make 'the poor' a touchstone of sensitivity to and obedience to the will of God. Is this to suggest, what Jesus Christ as the powerless embodiment of the power and love of God confirms, that the creative possibilities of reconciliation and hope in the present and the eventual fulfilment of love in the end lie with the powerless, with those who suffer, absorb, live, without counting for much or wielding so-called power? And does this suggest that really human development and liberation do not lie along the way of achieving affluence and power for everybody (a possibility so far off as to condemn most of the world to perpetual disappointment, frustration and a feeling of being left out of really human living)? It may be instead that we have to seek to promote an awareness of the power and possibility of living with a powerlessness and comparative poverty which is not degrading and frustrating but rather creative and human.

Of course there are immense difficulties here and the ideas and practices I am feeling after could easily be perverted in commending the status quo concerning both power and poverty. But this would be a most monstrous perversion. The question is simply: 'Where does the power which promotes love and human living really lie, and how do we respond to this power and make use of this power ourselves?' Christians are sharply and rightly re-discovering that the worship of God demands the service of men and the service of men requires involvement with society and *this* means concern with politics. But it does not follow from this that Christians have therefore to tackle the question of power by producing their own version of the power-game or deciding which side in any version of the power-game they ought to be aligned with. It might be that they have to decide how to take sides in the light of the fact that the Christian's basic alignment is always with and for the powerless and that it is the power of powerlessness, when taken up in suffering, absorption, reconciliation and love which is the one constantly creative and open-ended force at work in the world.

Thus far with my questions. At least they indicate why, before I began my outline of what I could perceive about a Christian's approach to violence, I wrote that I would later comment on what is implied by the extremely inadequate and unsatisfactory nature of these perceptions (p. 123). For, although I hope there is much contact, there is no satisfactory final fit between the six points which I have set out as my discussion and the questions which taking Jesus seriously 'as a real embodiment . . . of the presence and power of the Kingdom of God' seem to pose. This is an exceedingly important point. If we face the actual dilemmas which life brings, with the best insight and intuitions that are available to us, then we find that again and again it is not possible to be either truly human or truly Christian. To use violence is to be committed to a less than human activity which is bound to include inhuman effects among its results. To refrain from violence may be to side with and strengthen structures which, and people who, promote inhumanity. To pretend that Jesus justifies violence is to distort him and his record into our prejudices and dilemmas. Here we have a set of contradictions which have to be faced because to deny that they are contradictions is to contradict the value of human beings and the vision and promise indicated by Jesus. Each and every human being is worth love and not violence. Violence is always a violation of the human. Jesus embodies a way of love which suffers violence rather than endorses or licenses it. Violence is always a violation of the way of the love of God and Jesus. If this way does not exist and does not have adequate resources, then being human is finally contradicted. So we cannot and dare not explain away our practical dilemmas and contradictions with regard to violence, its occurrence, its use and its suffering. Violence is present, the use of violence may be chosen by us or forced upon us, but we cannot *justify* it. To do so is to deny humanity and to deny Jesus.

We must, therefore, live with the contradiction and know that it is contradiction. What is required and offered here is expressed very well in an article by Paul Oestreicher in *The Times* for Saturday April 12 1975, entitled 'Dietrich Bonhoeffer: Assassin or Saint?' In it he takes up the challenge of Desmond Tutu (now Dean of Johannesburg), who had enquired in a sermon in Westminster Abbey why Europeans venerated Bonhoeffer as a saint for being ready to join in a plot to assassinate Hitler while Africans resorting to the same methods are called violent terrorists. Oestreicher writes:

The current theology which sanctifies revolution is one easy way out of the double-think. It leaves Bonhoeffer's halo intact and turns wars of liberation into crusades. But it is not radical. . . . Bonhoeffer . . . knew that the Gospel's demand was to overcome evil with goodness; totally uncommon sense. For him, seeing no other practical alternative, the bitter paradox was his readiness to die as an assassin, throwing himself on God's forgiving grace. . . . Bonhoeffer himself divorced his complicity in the bomb plot from his ministry. He did not attempt to justify it theologically, let alone to sanctify it. He acted like an honest black Rhodesian friend of mine who simply says: 'For now, we've no choice but to put our Christianity into suspense.' Bonhoeffer would not have put it like that, but he had no illusions about the bitter and unresolved tensions between discipleship and political responsibility. But, living by grace, the tension did not break him. He acted when other good men were lost in prevarication.

He closes the article with this paragraph:

The dead of the First World War, the French Resistance a generation later, Bonhoeffer the failed assassin, the dead liberators of Zimbabwe and Namibia all, in their way, affirmed their humanity. They give us good cause for grateful remembrance. But 'following the martyred Son of God' was left to a tiny, mostly unsung number, like the Catholic peasant Franz Jägerstätter who, citing Jesus, refused to join Hitler's legions and went knowingly to the guillotine. There is room, with Christ in glory, not only for the obedient peasant but for the forgiven freedom-fighter and also for the many weak and bewildered characters like Peter and the rest of us. In God's mercy there is room too for the frightened tyrant who knows only dimly what he is doing.

Such an approach can itself remain humanizing realism and avoid degenerating into one more form of pious escapism only if at least two conditions are fulfilled. One is that the combination of tension, contradiction and hope sets one free for involvement with all its risks and costs and is not made a ground for prevarication, indifference or apathy. The other is that this vision of God which encourages one to talk about there being 'room with Christ in glory' and 'room in God's mercy' is based in reality. This returns us to the point which has had to be made explicit several times, namely that what is at issue is the basic nature of reality, of the energies and possibilities which are at work in the universe and of the resources which are available to us as human beings.

I hope that this discussion of violence may at least show why I am so concerned with contradictions and why I have found it necessary to insert the section on giving an explanation of the grounds and shape of the hope that is in us as Christians. My reason is twofold.

Firstly, it is plainly unrealistic to deny or explain away the contradictions in human behaviour, in the human condition and in the practice of any theory or set of insights which claim to embrace the realities of the world and to give men hope, whether this practice comes from

Marxism or from Christianity. Dialectic as a way of getting to grips with human and historical realities is insufficient. We do not proceed from a given or a thesis which is contradicted by an antithesis, out of which can be evolved a synthesis. Contradictions exist, remain real, and remain irreconcilable and irresolvable. To attempt to fit men and women into a dialectic which smooths away these contradictions is both specious and dangerous. It is specious because it is unrealistic. Violence does not become good or less contradictory of being human because it is, or is claimed to be, exercised on behalf of the poor or in the interests of liberation. It is at best ambiguous and it always does harm and provides the seeds of more harm. Violence may break up an intolerable situation, but it never solves anything. This was vividly symbolised for me recently when I saw a set of posters advertising a Mozambique liberation celebration. These posters were dominated by the sign of the liberation fighters, a sickle with, superimposed upon it, a sub-machine gun. But that sign was already hopelessly out of date. After guns assist in achieving freedom of a sort then problems have to be worked at which no violence can solve. Freedom from oppression feeds no one and give no one automatically any freedom for anything creatively human. Moreover, it is not only specious to try to fit men and women into a dialectic, it is also dangerous. Both sins and achievements then come to be evaluated by the theoretical roles in the dialectic of those who perform them. People performing the correct historical and class role can do no wrong and those performing false roles cannot have positive achievements. So true humanity is denied both in its wickedness and in its creativity.

All this follows if it is held that all contradictions in human living can ultimately be explained away or dealt with by a dialectical process, which transmutes them entirely into positive human good. The attempt to fit in and ultimately deny the contradictions scales them down and in so doing both the threats and the possibilities of being human are scaled down. But if real and irresolvable contradictions face us as human beings how can we have any ultimate hope in being human? We must be able to have a belief in reality which confronts these contradictions, lives with them and offers the hope of transcending them rather than resolving them. This is why the question of faith and of reality is so important. Hence we come to the second part of my twofold reason for concern with contradictions and with the ground and shape of the hope that is in us. That hope must proceed from a faith and an insight which is as tough and as realistic, and therefore as involved in doubt and in suffering, as are the contradictions which face us and in which we live.

We have to face contradictions of our human hopes and possibilities, expressed in our human behaviour and experienced in our human situations which do not and will not fit into any theory or practice about human beings and the world which is so far available to us. This applies to 'we' as human beings, from whatever perspective and with whatever faith or ideology we operate. But it applies especially to the 'we' who are Christians. Christians throughout the history of the church have claimed to have found 'Christian' solutions to the things that trouble our humanity. But they have not and we have not. Hence the starting-point for the whole exploration reflected in this book which lies in my increasing awareness that 'my' Christianity is contradicted by its historical record, its present social position and so much of the shape and behaviour of its present institutions. Hence also the position reached about violence and poignantly focused, as I believe, by the quotations from the article by Paul Oestreicher. There is no one clear Christian solution to the problem or problems of violence. It is rarely, if ever, possible to make a response to and in violence which can *justifiably* be called 'Christian', in the sense that it can clearly be shown to express and promote all that Jesus Christ stands for or calls us to. Further, and most importantly, this practical impossibility reflects a contradiction which is not only Christian but is also human. It is rarely, if ever, possible to make a response to and in violence which can *justifiably* be called 'human' in the sense that it can be shown to express and promote all that being human stands for or calls us to. There is always something actively inhuman and unchristian in violence. But, again, there is no clear and practical solution in practice for Christians which decisively deals with the inhuman and unchristian element. The contradiction remains and we have to live with it and through it.

We cannot, for example, proceed by giving ourselves the benefit of a doubt. We may (and many do) say that while violence must always worry us and make us doubtful, none the less it is justified when there is no other way to promote revolution and liberation. We may (and many do) say that while violence is always abhorrent and very doubtfully Christian, none the less it is on occasions justified by Jesus' commitment on the side of the oppressed and the poor. But it seems to me clear that we cannot and must not be given the benefit of this doubt. Violence is not justified even when it must be chosen or cannot be avoided. We have to accept the burden of sin and the contradiction involved and of which we become contributory parts. All of us are part of this solidarity in sin.

There is, therefore, no place for acting outside the contradictions and no practice which satisfactorily and finally overcomes them or guarantees the removal of them. Hope arises because faith reinforces the intuitions of love with the knowledge that God bears these burdens and contradictions with us and for us. But a faith which claims this knowledge of God must also be a faith which is ready to respond to and develop the knowledge claimed by openness to, and action in, the human possibilities and contradictions which make up being human now, in all their humanity and inhumanity. The contradictions are real and cannot be explained away. But it is the insight, the claim and the experience of faith that the energy and the presence of God unites with the possibilities of being human to give an ultimate promise of the contradictions being overcome and immediate foretastes now of freedom, renewal and love.

The Transcendence of God, which is the measure and the fulfilment of what men and women have it in them to be, is encountered for us in the midst of present possibilities and contradictions. We glimpse what men and women might be and deserve, as persons, to be. We know what we are and what actually happens to us. Between these two, the possibilities glimpsed and the actualities experienced, there is a gap which is bitter and tragic. This gap is not bridged by a theory, a dialectic or a process. It is a gap which has to be lived in and suffered with realism and hope. Of this realism and hope Jesus, with his cross and resurrection, is an effective symbol. The gap is realistically encountered. Rejection, suffering and death swallow him up. Resurrection comes after this encounter and represents the knowledge that his energy, power and purpose continue to be available for life after passing through rejection and death. Contradictions do not have to be ignored, explained away or accepted as defeats. They can be lived and suffered through. Thus we are not offered some total theory or explanation which ultimately shuts up human possibilities in an all-embracing totalitarianism. We have the chance of collaborating with an involved and suffering energy which can absorb and break through absolutely everything to an open and infinite freedom and fulfilment. Thus we have to take all the contradictions of human living and human society absolutely seriously and we are obliged to confront them and the conditions which produce them and which they promote with equal seriousness. For example, violence is to be struggled against and the conditions which produce and promote violence are to be combated. But neither the contradictions nor the combats and confrontations with what the contradictions represent are to be absolutized as defining what human living is or what human living can be.

It is for this reason that we have to be clear that, humanly speaking, not everything is politics. We need to be as clear about this as about the inevitability and necessity of political involvement and action. Both commitment and detachment are called for if we are to measure up to the whole range of human possibilities under God and to the whole spectrum of complexities and contradictions with which history confronts us. So the demands of a radical spirituality and a radical politics (see chapter 8) do not include the demand that everyone should at all times be involved in politics or should regard themselves as so involved. Being human is both more than politics and also possible in spite of politics. Nor will politics bring about the fulfilment of all legitimate human aspirations and possibilities.

It is not possible, however, to witness effectively against the absolutizing of politics unless one has realistically faced the ambiguity of politics. To be unrealistic about politics is to adopt a political stance which will almost always effectively support the political status quo. Thus naivety by Christians or Christian churches about politics is, in practice, irresponsible and, usually, reactionary. In the present situation of generally increasing political awareness such naivety may also reasonably be suspected of being disingenuous. It is, therefore, only out of political awareness and an attempt to be politically responsible that an authentic attempt can be made to make the humanly necessary witness to the limitation of politics. Hence, as I see it, the necessity for us Christians, and specially for us white bourgeois Christians, to be awakened to the contradiction of our Christianity and to the political implications and applications of this. Given that awareness, however, it is more than ever necessary to develop an appropriate awareness that politics should neither embrace nor determine everything.

Even the proper positive evaluation of politics has to be handled with care. There is some evidence that various Christian groups seek to overcompensate for previous neglect of political factors and activities by equating political involvement with the whole of Christian discipleship or by interpreting political programmes in largely biblical or traditional Christian terms. Such tendencies seem to deny the autonomy of the secular world and to be strangely redolent of the 'Christian imperialism' which Christians who show these tendencies are particularly concerned to attack and get rid of. It is by no means clear that everything has to be 'baptized' for it to be a proper work of God or an authentic human activity. Nor, I suspect, is it the job of the church as such or of Christians as such to be looking for a share in every activity of God in the world or in every piece of work that human beings legitimately undertake. God must be trusted and looked to to develop human affairs in his own way, a way which does full justice to the autonomy and diversity of human existence and human beings. Christians, presumably, no longer claim a monopoly in this way of God, however much they may cherish, and seek to respond to, the uniqueness of their calling to serve the God and Father of Jesus Christ and contribute to his purpose for all men. Thus while from the human point of view not everything is politics, from the Christian point of view there is no necessary calling to be involved in all the politics there are.

To maintain the possibility of a diversity of appropriate responses, both from a human and a Christian point of view, to the demands and the possibilities of political situations is indeed part of the witness to the limitations of politics which is humanly necessary. But it will always be necessary, also, to maintain a witness which goes further than that. Just as ignoring politics leads to human abuse, so does absolutizing politics. Therefore, part of taking politics absolutely seriously for the sake of being human will be the maintaining of a base, a belief and a vision from which it is possible to stand over against any political theory or action or set of relationships. This witness against politics is as much open to abuse as any commitment to politics. Insisting on ('our' version of) the spiritual can be just as much a way of gaining power over human beings or of ignoring their just demands as enforcing ('our' version of) the political. But this ubiquitous possibility of human abuse reinforces the necessity of maintaining a witness which reflects a reality which relativizes every human activity and achievement whatever. To be trapped within any current version of, or claim about, what it is to be human is to be dehumanized and to contribute to dehumanization.

Thus the existence of the church is a vital and necessary contribution to the development of humanization and the maintenance of a truly radical politics. This remains true however much the form of the existence of the church contradicts both the grounds of and the purpose for the church's existence. Indeed, the necessity and importance of the witness for which the church stands is underlined by these repeated occasions of contradiction. For the church exists to witness to the reality of God, as that reality is pointed to through Jesus Christ. This reality is known as a presence and energy who suffers the contradictions of human beings, as well as being both the source and the fulfilment of the possibilities of human beings. Thus the church can and must stand for the possibilities of Transcendence in the midst, despite its own contradiction of those possibilities. In so doing it points to and draws from a source of resources for sustaining tension, receiving repeated correction and experiencing renewal. The resources are available in the midst of realities which can neither be glossed out of contradiction nor forced into a shape which satisfies our humanness. Thus the maintenance of the possibilities of worship, of contemplation and of repentance are as important for being human as are the demands of politics, of justice and of freedom. If the contradictions of Christianity are taken as sufficient cause for the submergence of the possibilities of God into the possibilities of politics, then we are on our way to the final contradiction of humanity.

10

The Trinity – love in the end

So, one can argue until one is blue in the face, red in one's politics or grey with confusion and despair. The central question remains: 'What future can we work for and hope for – and what can we enjoy now?' This is the question of God, for the question of God is the question about what energies are at work in the whole of existence and experience and about how these energies are related to being human. Marx wrote: 'The criticism of religion disilllusions man so that he will think, act and fashion his reality as a man who has lost his illusions and regained his reason; so that he will revolve about himself as his own true sun. Religion is only the illusory sun about which man revolves so long as he does not revolve about himself' (quoted on p. 106 above). Given the contradictions of Christianity so far and the failures and threats of Marxism so far we may well ask whether there is any sun at all. To the criticism of religion there has to be added the criticism of revolution and the criticism of science. In practice and in history there are at least as many contradictions as creative achievements, as many threats as promises, as much suffering as enjoyment, as much death as fulfilment. (In view of current inhumanities and unhappiness I believe this to be an understatement. But everyone must judge for themselves.) Thus the criticism of religion, of revolution and of science (all surely deeply justified), may well 'disillusion man'. What then is left?

In the light of the glory of God revealed in Jesus and sustained by the Spirit, everything is left. All the grounds for criticism and disillusionment, all the incidents and processes of contradiction, all the valid insights and promises of religion, all the just protests and human hopes of revolution, all the achievements and skills of science. Men and women are offered the resources for affirming and developing their humanity in the midst of all these things, together with a promise and vision of fulfilment beyond all these things. The reality and the realism of this promise and of this vision can be established only in the attempt to respond to the possibilities they suggest and to live by the resources which they offer. Neither God nor our humanity can be established *a priori* by definition in advance. We have to live into both. Hence such hints about the practice of hopeful human living as can be obtained from this account of an exploration are to be found chiefly in the chapters about giving an account of the faith in us, pursuing radical spirituality and radical politics, and living with violence and contradictions. But the practice of hopeful living requires motivation, sustenance, correction and inspiration. It must be able to stand up to reality. In what hope, by what vision and with what resources do we live with and in the human and historical realities which we have been considering all through this exploration and which will go on being the context of our lives and our deaths?

The most realistic answer that can be given to this question is that we live in the hope of God, we live by the vision of God and we live with the resources of God. This has been the answer which has been touched on, implied or illustrated at various points throughout the wanderings of this book. For its final section and to serve, as it were, as a temporary resting-place where this account of a part of an exploration can come to an end and from which the next stage of an exploration and pilgrimage can go on, I want to consider the doctrine or symbol of the Trinity. I want to do this because the 'doctrine' of the Trinity reflects and represents the discovery of the possibilities of being human through a developing experience of the shape of the activities of God towards us and among us. I put the word 'doctrine', referring to the Trinity, into inverted commas because it is not a wholly suitable word for designating the status and nature of the human conceptual entity or composition which is referred to as 'the Trinity'. 'Doctrine' has come to suggest something too intellectualistic, formal and cut and dried. For example, a sentence like 'God is a trinity of persons' can be taken as something like an axiom in a theoretical description of God (or 'doctrine of God') which provides a blueprint, authorized by revelation, which prescribes what we are to believe about God and how we are to understand this belief.

'The Trinity' however, is much more of a symbol or icon. It has been the subject of much doctrinal discussion and reflects the insights gained and clarified in those discussions. But it operates as an articulated picture with a worked out, recognized and traditional pattern which continues in use as a focus for and a provocation of experience. The shape and pattern of this icon was worked out to present and represent a living possibility. This was (and is) glimpsed in experience and passed on in believing and worshipping communities by means of images, words and actions. The whole process is kept alive by the activity and presence of the reality (that is, God) to whom the symbol points and the pattern of whose activity the symbol reflects. Thus 'the Trinity' stands, not for a doctrine but for a way of life which is related to God's life. To reduce 'the Trinity' to doctrine or to metaphysics is to shrink its significance in a deadly way. 'Deadly' is not too strong a term to use, for the insight symbolized and maintained by the icon of the Trinity, with its doctrinal and metaphysical implications, is nothing less than the confident discovery that the possibilities of men and women *are* the possibilities of God.

Thus the Trinity is the summing-up and focusing symbol of the decisive experiences of Transcendence in the midst which not only authorize but compel us to 'maintain the impossible possibility that love will achieve fulfilment' (see p. 79 above). Again and again during the various experiences and efforts of reflection which lie behind this book and throughout the attempt to compose first lectures and then a book for publication, a recurring question for me has been: 'But why struggle to point to and argue for something that is so fantastically visionary and so beyond all reasonable expectation as the kingdom of the God who is symbolised by the Trinity with its formalized shape of "Father, Son and Holy Ghost" ?'

I have given some account of the basis for this attempt in chapter 6 where I have tried to describe the fellowship of knowledge of experienced and renewed realities which constitutes and enables Christian believing in and through history. But I need now, in connection with this attempt to outline the significance of the symbol of the Trinity, to give a rather different account of the hope that is in me. I cannot get away from the attempt to respond to the kingdom of God and to live into the possibilities symbolized by the Trinity because of a simple conviction about love.

It is neither fantastically visionary nor beyond all reason to take the risk and the hope of commitment to a vision which speaks of a community and a communion where love fulfils love so that everyone is fully human because everyone is fully human. What we occasionally glimpse and occasionally experience in and through the faces of our fellow human beings and in and through relationships with them compels us to take love absolutely seriously. The vision and understanding of God which is symbolized by the Trinity sets us free to take love absolutely seriously. Thus the motivation for continuing to try to make sense of the realities symbolized by the kingdom of God and the Trinity is the compulsion of love reinforced by the freedom of love. Men and women require love. God offers love. Here is the opportunity of making sense in a collaboration which makes sense of us, of achieving fulfilment in a working together which both is and produces fulfilment. The place where this sense has to be sought after and this fulfilling begun is wherever men and women are concerned with themselves, their neighbours and their enemies. Hence the incessant need, until history is ended, to incarnate the compulsion of love and the freedom of love in the ambiguities, contradictions and possibilities of particular human living and dying.

But the symbol of the Trinity focuses the discovery that God is already that pattern and energy of fulfilling and relating love which we require to receive, and to be contributory parts of, if our humanness is to be fulfilled. (We have to remember that love, taken absolutely seriously, makes it clear that no one can be fully human until all are fully human. There can be no final enjoyment and achievement of the kingdom until the flow of love is such that we live 'from each according to his capacity, to each according to his need'.) Thus, in this discovery of the pattern of God's activity towards us and among us, we are given also the promise of the pattern of the final future. In the ultimate future there lies the pattern and the energy of this fulfilling love. But this energy of God is not only the shape of the future, it is also that which is at work shaping this future. Hence the incarnate possibilities of eternal love and eternal humanness in every 'here and now'. It is the incipient relationships of love, together with their struggles, achievements and sufferings, which have a future commensurate with the possibilities and promises of being human. Nothing else does. Anything else would shape up men and women in that which is less than fully human. Thus, what the Trinity symbolizes is the establishment and vindication of an ultimate insight of love and an ultimate evaluation of love. Human beings have infinite possibilities of relationship and enjoyment which are to be eternally established. That is what the love of this mother for this child, of this man for that woman, of this comrade for that fellow fighter or seeker is about. Hence we live between heaven and hell and not in some lesser or more manageable dialectic or process, whether scientifically or historically describable. Our fates are often unmanageable or intolerable because our destinies are as infinite as our possibilities.

The Trinity as a symbol with a formalized shape of its own serves to direct attention to the shape or form of a corporate and extended experience of God which reflects the pattern of God's activities towards us. It is thus a symbol of what has been discovered and a provocation to sharing in this discovery and to being part of extending the implications and applications of the discovery. Hence a brief account of the emergence and shaping of this symbol may serve, as I have already said, as a temporary resting-place suitable for bringing to an end this account of a section of an exploration. It could be suitable as giving some indication of an interpenetration of reality, experience and vision which lends weight to the conviction that the immediately preceding paragraphs are not rhetoric, fantasy or romanticism but point to actual possibilities of historical human existence arising from experience. It should be suitable as avoiding any sense of a climax which summarizes and synthesizes all the threads and investigations of our exploration and overcomes the contradictions we have been considering. High points or visions of wholeness and hope are not things which arise in the human exploration to order, or at controlled stages after so many chapters, episodes or attempts. They are discovered as gifts in the midst of our living and struggling and they have to be followed out and followed up once again in the midst. So, finally, an account of the shaping of the symbol of the Trinity should also be suitable as a place at which to leave this exploration, because such an account should at least make it clear that we are concerned with energy to be responded to and an openness to be entered into. The Trinity is a symbol for pilgrims who know no limits to their hopes of endurance, discovery and enjoyment.

The account which now follows assumes the argument in chapter 6 about the possibilities of knowing that can arise from being in fellowship with living realities through a continuing community. It also assumes the argument outlined in chapter 2 about the development of Israel's understanding of themselves, their God and the role and possibilities of their future all together in the demands and offers of events and circumstance (see pp. 21 f.). This particular starting-point is essential because the basic elements which give rise to the doctrine and symbol of the Trinity are twofold. First, there is the belief in and experience of the God of Israel who is also the God of Jesus. Secondly, there is the impact of Jesus himself within the context of the faithful life of Israel as reflected in what we Christians now call 'the Old Testament'. In accordance with the approach outlined in both chapter 2 and chapter 6 I am working on the conviction that we receive the witness to these two realities (the God of Israel and Jesus himself) through the communal experience and reflection of the two realities and that this witness is rekindled in continuing communal experience. Thus the account I am giving is an account of what believers have discovered about that which they believe in. I have already argued (again in Chapter 6) why an account has to be given 'from inside'. The book as a whole should show, and this account as it proceeds should reinforce this showing, why what is discovered 'from inside believing' demands a continual engagement and dialogue with 'what is outside', that is, with the world as a whole and humanity at large.

Thus the symbol of the Trinity develops from taking seriously that experience and understanding of the God of Israel and of Jesus which was undergone and developed by those who became followers of this God 'through' or 'in' Jesus. Our basic evidence for this experience and this understanding lies in the Bible. For those of us who are fellow believers the Bible thus offers reliable material for pointing to experience, for promoting experience and for correcting experience. This reliable material is offered from within the experience of believers and it is offered to the experience and response of believers. Knowing, testing and practising have, as always, to go together and to affect one another. A constant attempt to take the biblical material seriously in its own shapes and authenticity is a necessary part of the corporate knowledge of living realities which faith keeps alive in the world and which keeps faith alive both in the world and, when necessary, over against the world.

If we attempt to take the biblical material seriously in this way, then we have to give full weight both to the logic of the mythology which is found in the biblical presentations and to the self-understanding of the believing communities as it is reflected in the documents. To be ready to take the logic of a mythology seriously we have to be liberated from the notion that both logic and reality are defined by and confined to some combination of history and science (where 'science' is to be understood in its Anglo-Saxon sense, as scientifically established knowledge of the natural universe; for some reason or other the Anglo-Saxons are particularly narrow in their notions of 'science'. But that is matter for another inquiry). However it has, I hope, been made sufficiently clear at various points in this exploration that we are wrestling with conflicting claims about the nature of reality and the energies and possibilities open to us. It is therefore possible perhaps, to draw attention to this point once again and just continue with the exposition. In doing so it is also necessary to reiterate that there is no intended suggestion that history or science should be taken less seriously. The struggle is to ensure that history and science are taken less absolutely, because to absolutize them is not appropriate to the possibilities of being human. Nor is it appropriate to the nature of historical events and trends or to scientifically established facts and processes themselves. In the midst of nature and history human beings are open to a transcendence which goes beyond the present conditions of our existence. Thus our concern is always to wrestle with and to explore human possibilities rather than to limit them.

Hence the logic of a mythology which insists on taking both science and history seriously within the story which the mythology tells, may well turn out to be a far more appropriate guide for human living and human hoping. This of course, can be so only if that logic insists that the story told by the mythology interpenetrates at all points with the realities of life as we live them and experience them and reflects a truly interpenetrating reality. Given this, a story about what it is and what it will be to be human is far more humanly appropriate than any scientific account. First, all scientific accounts are within the human story anyway. We are only just beginning to rediscover how arbitrary and impoverishing a thing it is to allow any one, or a selection of them, to claim to determine the whole story in their own terms. Secondly, a story is always open until it is ended, there are possibilities of a great variety of interpretations which will enrich the story and men and women can make their own contributions to what a story means and how it is to be taken. Further, if it could be taken seriously that our human existence is, or can be, very like the taking part in a story, then we might have very powerful resources for resisting any attempt to 'fix' the story so that everybody was forced into playing, for example, Marxist roles, or, for that matter, so-called Christian ones. The question, once again, is that of the final nature of the reality of which we are part and with which we have to do.

The writers of the Bible, and those who are reading them with a shared faith and experience, are dealing with images, stories, arguments and testimonies which reflect the shape of experiences and which are offered as shaping experience so that the realities testified to may be entered into by others who will then be able to offer their own testimony to these same realities. Thus, there emerges within this interaction of testimonies to experience and experience itself the story about the world (in fact about men, God and the world) which the believers hold themselves to be authorized to tell. This is also the story of which they are part and to which they are called to contribute. If we take the logic of this biblical mythology seriously, then it is clear that none of the stories in the Bible nor the overall trend of the whole has any sense or coherence without God as the objective reality and interpenetrating reality who is the main actor in the whole story. Further, this claim and presentation of the story (that God is the principal actor in the story of men and the world, a claim mythological in form but about *reality*) is reinforced if we take seriously the worship of 'the people of God'. At its heart this is understood to be, and experienced as, the living experience of the living God. Worship is not an 'as if' activity and experience, and the biblical story is not presenting the claim that the world is 'as if' God were the principal actor and energy in it. The biblical story is the claim that worship is the clue to existence, to activity and to hope. This is why hope is realistically infinite and the 'impossible possibility' of love is known to be the proper and realistic insight into, and evaluation of, the possibilities of being human.

Within this story, and as a decisive contribution to the development of this story, we have the varying presentations of the New Testament about Jesus, including the often enigmatic and differing presentations in the four gospels. Yet, differing and difficult as these presentations may be, there is a logic or shape in them which makes the Trinitarian question, if not the Trinitarian symbol, inevitable. This is so because the presentations taken as a whole will not permit the fitting of Jesus into any set of categories taken from the concepts, experiences or traditions unaffected by the impact associated with Jesus himself. Neither the logic of these records nor the self-understanding and life of the community presenting these records are satisfied by a proposed account of, or response to, Jesus which includes him wholly in a class with other men and women, however rare or highly valued. There is an awkwardness, a standing-out about him which is reflected in terms of eschatology, of transcendence, of strange otherness.

Thus what came to be known technically as the 'christological question' is inherent from the beginning of any stories about Jesus, is indeed inherent in the fact that there is any telling of these stories at all. The question is a basic one about his acting and his living. It is simply the question 'Who is this?', 'What authority does his existence have?' The answer given by the New Testament in various ways associates him uniquely and awkwardly with God. The New Testament thus contains a series of arguments or propositions about the story which is to be told about God, man and the world in the light of Jesus. What expectations can be authentically developed and how are these to be maintained?

Jesus is received and presented as the servant of the God of Israel who is the God of the whole earth. He is, in some way, uniquely associated with this God's authority, presence, power and purpose. The decisive episode which reveals the particular quality of the 'uniqueness of the uniqueness' of Jesus is that which is traditionally referred to as cross and resurrection. There is no way of getting round the fact that this episode, with its series of events, is both believed and claimed to be a set of historical events which are unique in history. The conflicts and claims about the nature of ultimate reality come to their sharpest focus here. As the apostle Paul is portrayed as asking before King Agrippa in

Jerusalem, 'Why should it be thought a thing incredible with you, that God should raise the dead ?' (Acts 26.8, AV). The conflict is not about whether the evidence for one particular event having happened is good enough, but about the ultimate nature of reality because of the reality which is encountered in Jesus, as highlighted by the events which surrounded his crucifixion and which evoked the first knowledge of his resurrection. We are confronted, through the records of the New Testament and through the testimonies presented by those who first became 'Christian', with a series of stories which make sense of the events and an account of the events which create the stories. The logic of these stories, and that which gives them their point and the purpose for telling them, is the discovery of the unique and decisive role and status of the principal actor in the historical story, that is, of Jesus. In the telling of the story this discovery becomes indicated and focused by what emerges as the principal event in the story, that is, the resurrection.

The question which persists (of course to this day) is about how and in what way the events are unique. This is related to the question of what story may or must be consequently told about them. (As we should say, within the tradition, what is the good news or gospel which rises from them ?) And this is related to the question of what sort of story the world with its processes and its histories is shown to be and, consequently, of how we may play our part in the story and what we may expect to receive from it and within it. The answer to all these questions depends on the status and role of the principal actor in the 'Christian' story, that is to say, Jesus, in relation to the author, finisher and principal actor of the whole story, that is to say, God. The various stories and presentations in the New Testament either imply or specifically state (in a variety of ways) that the 'Jesus story' is of cosmic significance. Against the background of the commitment, worship and suffering of the first Christian communities, we have to ask ourselves how writers could dare to produce such things as the meditation about hope and the groaning of the whole of creation in Romans 8, the claim about everything being held together in Jesus as God's Son in Colossians (cf. Col. 1.17 etc.), the expectation of 'all in heaven and on earth' being 'headed up' into a unity with Christ described in Ephesians (cf. Eph. 1.10) or the historical poetic prose of the prologue to John's gospel (John 1.1–18) with its weaving together of the structures of the universe, the history of the Jews and the particular events of the life of Jesus.

The logic of the mythology is pretty clear. We are being told that the reality expressed in and through the life of Jesus is the reality offered to us in the light of which we have to see all reality and out of which we are to receive strength to live into reality and be part of making reality. Such a story and such an approach to reality has to make its way in and through the context and the content of actual human lives and will not be maintained without the sort of continuing community knowledge discussed in chapter 6. Further, the knowledge of such a story demands the same sort of incarnation in living and dying as the story tells about. Unless there is a continuing attempt to live according to the story and to discover its truth in practice, then it becomes nothing but a story and so loses that grip on reality which is the whole point and aim of the story. It may well be a common axiom of both Marxism and spirituality that there is no effective theory without praxis. This is why the issue of contradictions is so urgent. And the reason for returning to the basic story in the face of and in the midst of these contradictions lies in a conviction arising from the hearing of the story and an attempt to live by it and into it. This is the conviction that the question of the incredibility of God's raising of the dead and the problem of the incredibility of love are one and the same. The story of the discovery and rediscovery of the resurrection is the story of the discovery and rediscovery that the whole of love is fulfillable – and this in reality. Hence this is the story which can be lived by and so must be lived out in the face of all failures, contradictions and deaths.

The Trinity is the symbol which emerged as pointing to and defending the reality of this story and as setting forth how this story enables us to respond to and live in reality. The living pattern of the story in the New Testament and of the faith, vision and life which is reflected in and enabled by the story is that of God (known to Jesus as 'Father'), Jesus and the Spirit. This pattern emerges because the story does not hold together either as dynamic vision or as dynamic life and process without these activities and foci. The first is the overruling energy and presence of the transcendent God who is both the God of Israel and the God of the whole earth. The second is the historic energy and activity of Jesus, who he was, what he did and what was undergone by him and revealed through him in the episode of cross and resurrection. The third is the immanent activity of the Spirit continuing the story, developing the story, maintaining the knowledge of the story in actual communities and relating the implications of the story to living in touch with concrete realities. The living of the people who came to understand themselves as 'Christian' was thus bound to produce the question of how the three activities who hold together in the story, and whose holding together in fact constitutes the story, hold together in reality. So Christian believing and living required and requires wrestling with what may seem to be a highly theoretical and metaphysical question about the articulation and coherence of the vision and knowledge of God, Jesus and the Spirit. In fact, this is a very practical concern, for it is about the nature of the story-creating reality and the impact of the reality-creating story of which we find ourselves to be a part.

In the first place, questions of this type are clearly questions for and in Christian communities. But the very content of the story makes these questions into questions about the hopes and expectations of being human for all men and women and has to do with the possibilities available throughout this world and beyond. The question about the being and significance of Jesus is the same as the question about the being and significance which we can expect through or because of him. The question about the being and significance of the Spirit is the same as the question about what is at work in reality to enable us to be human and therefore about what sort of humanity we can expect to enjoy. This is why arguments which were first recognized in coherently formulated forms in the so-called 'Arian' conflicts of the fourth century are perennial and have an importance far wider than the currency or credibility of the particular sets of technical terms in which they are formulated.

The Arians of the fourth century argued that the reality which constituted Jesus and was at work in him had to be sharply and decisively distinguished from the divine reality. There was a parallel argument about the Spirit which was denied to be directly and decisively divine. The fourth-century form of this struggle crystallized around the famous or notorious Greek words *homo-ousios* and *homoi-ousios*. The former was developed to maintain that the constituent reality of God, of Jesus and of the Spirit was one and the same, while the latter indicated that the realities were similar. A debate in such terms clearly provides splendid material for irony from later commentators. Here were the self-styled followers of the God of universal love at loggerheads over an iota and, in any case, swapping metaphysical niceties which could have no anchorage in either particular practice or wider reality. From the point of view of the Christian story, however, the issue was and is, one that makes literally all the difference in the world. It is of a piece with the incredibility of the resurrection and the incredibility of love.

For the object and effect of 'Arian-type' arguments is to keep apart the divine and fulfilling reality in its unique real and full sense from the material and historical which is the arena of human activity and hope. The direct and unmediated presence and activity of God in the world, as we know it, live it and are part of it, is denied. But this is to tell a different story about God, human beings and the world from the story arising out of the impact of Jesus and of the story about him in relation to the God known to him as Father. It is therefore to have a different understanding of the possibilities both of God and of man.

This determination to keep God and history apart, and this denial of the unambiguous commitment of divine activity and presence to the world and to our human reality, was very much in keeping with the current thought patterns of the Mediterranean world of the early centuries of Christianity. It was in keeping also with the strong pressures to dualism which have played a great part in developing (and distorting) many doctrinal and ethical positions, including Christian ones, from that time to the present. Such a denial is, however, contrary to the essential shape and dynamism of the God/Jesus/Spirit interrelation which is to be seen at work in and reflected through the New Testament and the subsequent faith and life of continuing Christian communities. To be faithful to the worship of these communities, to the faith and shape of their corporate understanding, and to the story they had learnt to tell and be part of, it was necessary to affirm both the fullness and the directness of God in Jesus. A parallel affirmation was required to maintain the fullness and directness of the energy and activity of God as the Spirit, the continuing immanent activity of the power and purpose embodied in Jesus.

A formula emerged as a symbol of these affirmations and as a protective summary of what had been learnt about the possibilities of God and man. The traditional form in English of this Greek formula is the statement that God is 'three persons in one substance'. The meaning of this formula arises out of the questions and the experience which gave rise to it. It is a technical and formalized formula worked out in order to both make and safeguard certain assertions about reality which have emerged from experience and experiment and which are intended as encouragements to further experience and experiment. It is the symbol of a faith to live by, discovered out of living, and proclaiming the offer of a life to be received and lived. The formula has a reference beyond history but our concern with it has to be deeply historical because it was discovered in history, is about history and has meaning for our understanding and hopes of history. The first assertion, as I have already indicated, is that God and the world in which we develop or lose our humanness are not to be kept apart. This is symbolized in the 'one substance' part of the formula. The presence and activities of Jesus as a man and the presence and activities of the Spirit in the process of the world and the aspects of human beings are the presence and activity of God and this is so in the fullest possible sense (that is, in the sense in which God is God and not in some diluted sense with which we may think we can cope intellectually).

The 'three persons' part of the formula has a symbolic function which complements the 'one substance' component. By insisting on 'the distinction of the persons' (three persons rather than one) the symbol is asserting that the different levels, modes or media at which or in which we experience God all have their own dependent but authentic reality. To use the formula of the 'three persons' is to assert the reality of God, the reality of human beings and the reality of the world and history all in their own proper way. In order to explain this further it is first necessary to make it clear that, in the formula or symbol 'three persons in one substance', the term 'person' refers to existent realities (with stress on the reality of this existence or these existences) and not to personality, still less to 'personalities'. This may be unfortunate, mis-leading or even annoying. But whatever we may mean in modern parlance by the term 'person', it is certain that, in the formula, 'three persons in one substance', the term 'person' is not used in the way in which we normally (or abnormally) use that word. In the formula, the English term 'person' is simply the Latin term *persona* which, in its turn, replaced or translated the Greek term *hypostasis*. Now when this formula came into existence (the fourth century AD) the term *hypostasis* could not mean any of our meanings of 'person' because they had not been evolved – indeed, the doctrine or symbol of the Trinity played a signi-ficant part in the development of the notion both of the person and of personality. But to this I shall briefly return shortly. The point at the moment is the role of the term 'three persons' in the formula 'three persons in one substance' presented as a picture and assertion about God and therefore as a symbol making or guarding an assertion about reality as a whole. Here it is necessary to be clear about the implications of the formula being a 'technical and formalized' one, as I pointed out above. The terms take their meaning from being in the formula and from the usage and experience which threw up the formula. Thus, in this formula, the term 'person' does not point in the direction of what we currently mean by person, personality or personhood, but in the direction of existence and reality.

What is being asserted or symbolized, therefore, is the validity and significance of the threefold form of the experience of God which shapes the story about God, man and the world which Christians are author-ized to tell. For example, the divine 'person' who constitutes the energy and involvement of the human personality Jesus must be thought of and symbolized as distinct from the divine 'person' whom Jesus addresses as 'Father'. If this were not so, then the whole human and historical story of which Jesus is the principal and defining actor would be a sham. Or else it would be a divine masquerade which made humanity and history a sham. But both the story of creation and the story of Jesus are clearly concerned to maintain that history and being human are to be taken wholly seriously in their own right and that it is out of history that human beings develop to receive their divine fulfilment. Similarly and analogously, the activity and the presence of the Spirit must be thought of as a 'person' distinct from the 'person' of both the Father and the Son. To have no room for distinctiveness in the symbol would be to leave us no room for the discrete realities of history and time, and the sequences in the story of the encounter of God and man would become unreal and unhistorical. Further, the activity of the Spirit in, and in association with, the processes of nature and history and with the living of human beings would be to absorb them into God rather than to unite them to him. In the case of human beings, this would be to deny ultimate value to personality and to the infinite worth of persons.

Thus the symbol of the Trinity insists on and lays claim to a unique way of holding together Transcendence and immanence, eternity and history, God and human beings. This, it proclaims, is the necessary and legitimate interpretation of the experienced and perceived story of God, Jesus and the Spirit and of the story which therefore follows about God, man and the world. The dependent and temporary realities of nature and history, and of the conditions of human living within them, are in no way diminished as to their autonomy, authenticity and significance by the commitment of God to them and the involvement of God in them. At the same time God is neither defined nor limited by his un-limited involvement and his unambiguous commitment. He is Tran-scendence known to us as Transcendence in the midst.

He is also known as love. The symbol of the Trinity represents and reinforces this knowledge in a particularly powerful way. For the symbol insists that the energy and activity of Jesus is the energy and activity of God, while at the same time insisting on the fully human and historical reality of this personality and his story. What is true of Jesus is true of God. We have therefore a statement, a claim, a recognition about infinite care expressed in the sharing in abysmal cost. Suffering and death are not thereby given meaning. But they are shown to be part of that which is engaged in by the divine. They are therefore known to be part of that which may be engaged in with human hope. Love is known to be engaged with the impossibility and the contradiction of love. Further, the symbol of 'three persons in one substance' also declares that it is proper to think of relationships as part of the pattern and dynamic of ultimate reality. Love which is expressed and enjoyed as communion and community is thus the pattern of the final future, just as it is the underlying energy at work in the present and the initial energy which has been at work from the beginning. We are both authorized and commanded to live, hope, suffer and celebrate, in the midst of all that comes to us, in the conviction that it is the relationships of love which have a future commensurate with the possibilities of being human. Nothing else fulfils the forces and potentialities of human beings. Anything else can and will become idolatry and inhumanity.

The Trinity thus symbolizes the discovering of love which is both transcendent and committed to being at work in history and in human beings. This is the discovery which is reflected and reported in the stories the Bible records about God and about Jesus and therefore about God, man and the world. Hence love is known to be essentially committed to collaboration in the construction of reality for eternity. Men and women are shown to be pilgrims and workers who have their own share in the creation and development of their own history. We are part of, and co-operators in, both the telling and the making of the story which will end in the community and communion of the life of God poured out into the life of men and of the whole universe. Marx was perfectly right to speak of the opportunity for man to 'think, act and fashion his reality as a man'. But this opportunity does not come to man as 'his own sun'. Such a mistaken turning inwards is diminishing, destructive and dehumanizing. What the Trinity points us to and calls us to is the emergence and the establishment of human being, human selfhood and human personality as central to the possibilities and purposes of the universe. There is the possibility of a universal giving to all men and women by all men and women taken up into, and as part of, the love and the life of God. Personal experience and historical activity are vindicated as the places where men and women have the opportunity to enter upon and contribute to a becoming human which has no end save in the fulfilment of love by love.

The Trinity, therefore, is the symbol of the shape and the shaping of an unfinished story. The full significance of this story cannot be known until the end is achieved and to be enjoyed. The symbol itself, therefore, must be taken as a prescription for the direction in which we may look and search for understanding and experience. It is not to be taken, as dogmatically it has often been, as a description which determines what we may understand or experience. As I wrote earlier, 'the Trinity is a symbol for pilgrims who know no limits to their hopes of endurance, discovery and enjoyment' (p. 145). God cannot be described, he can only be pointed to and responded to. One currently important example of the effect of this understanding of the role and status of the symbol is to be found with regard to its traditional form of 'God, Father, Son and Holy Spirit'. We are now steadily accumulating evidence about the negative as well as the positive effects of the resonances of the term 'Father'.

Given the pattern of the living of Jesus as portrayed in the gospels, it was inevitable that the name of, or term for, the 'first person' of the Trinity should be 'Father'. Moreover, this usage reflects and points to a great wealth of creative experience and hope about the reality of God and of his activity towards us. This wealth includes the confident dependence of Jesus himself which was so clearly the source which enabled the establishment of his identity and the fullness of his freedom. He not only related to God as 'Abba' but also gave his disciples the courage to pray 'Our Father'. Thus he invited them, and so us, to a like dependence, identity and freedom. Now, however, we have a great deal of evidence about the pathological workings of the father-figure concept. There is a dependence which is crippling and demeaning, identity is distorted and freedom is paralysed. The males among us are just beginning to learn from the articulations of our feminine fellow human beings what the exaltation of masculinity has meant, and is meaning, to half the human race. Theologians from Africa and elsewhere are beginning to demonstrate how hierarchical paternalism has been used, explicitly or implicitly, to justify Western domination over 'colonial' people and their cultures. We have, therefore, an immense amount to learn, through suffering, celebration and change, about what it is to be human and about what is offered us from the being and energy of God. Certainly, what is offered will be received only as we face up to the contradictions of identity and freedom which are now being exposed. How we shall name the God who is love when we have travelled a good deal further in our human pilgrimage and struggle I see no way of guessing or knowing. The pattern which points to Transcendence, to Jesus and to the Spirit and which symbolizes love in the beginning, in the midst and in the end will, however, remain.

It is clear then that the story has yet to be lived and to be told. A discussion and description of the symbol of the Trinity can therefore be put forward as a suitable resting-place at which to bring to an end an account of a piece of Christian and human exploring. For we can always rest in God and in what we have so far received from him and of him. But the resting-place is itself an invitation to further receiving and a starting-point for further exploration. We return to the contradictions and to the possibilities, to the sufferings and to the promises. If we are to respond to all that goes on around us and within us, we must seek to know all we can. If we are to respond to what we glimpse in other human beings and what we receive from other human beings, we must love all we can. Confronted by the contradiction of Christianity and by the contradiction of humanity I still find that I need to know and to love. The Trinity points to the possibility and the promise that in reality and in the end knowing and loving are one and the same. St Augustine and many others have known this and hoped this but it is always necessary to struggle through to our own glimpses and then to seek to be sustained in following them up. The point of attempting a summary and piece-meal account of the emergence of the symbol of the Trinity is simply to make it clear that, like the contradictions, the Vision is found in human history and experience. The Vision therefore, has to be obeyed and received in human history and experience. We must face contradictions in living, struggle in politics and search for spirituality. None of these things must be held apart and in striving to bring them together we are striving also to receive and be part of the offer of being human which is 'through Jesus Christ'.

The symbol of the Trinity reminds us that the offer which Jesus Christ makes is the offer of his Father; that is to say the offer of the life of God, Father, Son and Holy Spirit. The place of the final fulfilment of the offer is 'in God', that is to say, not in history but in the God who initiates history, lives in history, fulfils history and transcends history. God has, and is, his own place and being. He does not depend upon us or history or the universe for being God. But his activity in history, his presenta-tion of himself in and as Jesus Christ and his constant suffering and struggle with men in and as the Spirit makes it clear that his transcendent way of being is not remote, tyrannical or self-preserving. Rather the very energy of his being is love. Therefore it is clear that although God can be God without man and that God *is* God without man, none the less God *will not* be God without men. He does not need us. He loves us.

The trinitarian picture of God warns us against creating God in our own image and helps us to fight against our inveterate tendencies to seek to define or delimit God in terms of our tribalisms and contradictions. With him there is no pathology of identity, for all that he is sets him perfectly and absolutely free for an eternal activity of identification with his creatures. We who are concerned to know and follow him are constantly creating contradictions by defending God and by picturing him and responding to him as if he were a defensive God. His wrath must be appeased, so even torture has been justified in his name. His rules must be kept, so offensive moralisms limit and degrade men and women. His name must be protected, so he is claimed for Christian mission or Christian church but it is a threat or an offence to have to recognize him at work at large, unconditioned and unconditionally. But all this is, in the strictest sense of the term, theological non-sense, a denial of the reality that God is and of the sense which he is offering to make of the world and of us.

This nonsense he is constantly giving himself to overcome. One of the ways in which he does this is to make manifest the contradictions of the Church and the churches so that we may recognize our blatant practical denials of him and learn ways of once more becoming part of his continuous work among men. He offers us opportunities for the breaking down of cultural and class tribalisms, used to keep some men and women less human than others. He encourages us by the breaking out of diverse riches in men and women of all cultures and races. He invites us to take part in the breaking through of neighbourly love and of revolutionary humanism. Above all he is present in the suffering of man's inhumanity to man.

The Trinity is not only the symbol of this supreme identity which is love and therefore free for all identifying and for every suffering which the winning of full human identity requires. The shape of the trinitarian symbol also indicates that in the end identity is not to be had at the cost of other identities but by being the fulfilment of them. For the symbol indicates a dynamic interdependence which is perfect identity and perfect freedom. For example, the Son is to be understood as the Father's way of being himself and expressing himself in the historical reality and person of Jesus. Thus, in the Trinity there is a picture of a total interpenetration of being and activity which provides and sustains a total identity which works precisely for mutual identifying. It is, in fact, a perfect model of and promise for personality, and for personality as all-fulfilling and all-embracing. What this picture promises us is that there is a way of my being me which will come about by my finding my being in you. And that this will come about when and as you are you and I am I. The proper diversity of tribalisms and of individualities will contribute to the enrichment of a mutual union.

The pattern of this promise is also the pattern of the energy which is at work to enable all human beings to develop collaboratively as the neighbour to all other human beings. The Trinity is therefore also the symbol of the perfect society. For it points to that community of relationship where all will fulfil one another in communion, communication and true communism. Here we can have no lasting city. Our hope lies in this final fullness. But it is here and now that we have to learn to love and to hope. Thus we are returned to the practice of radical politics and radical spirituality and to the facing of our contradictions.

It is at least clear that we who are Christians must be contradicted to repentance if we are to play the part offered by God in the redemption of history and the salvation of men and women. It is only through a radical repentance worked out in terms of a radical politics and a radical sprituality that we can search for a living which will be in any way faithful to God, Father, Son and Holy Spirit and to the love which human beings plainly evoke, display and need.

Index